PROF.* DAMAN DEV SOOD, FBCI, FBCS, CBCI

Director – DBD Training & Consultancy (OPC) Private Limited

IEEE Ambassador

Past Chair – IEEE Computer Society Delhi Section Chapter

Member Champion – IEEE India MOVE,

Partner Relations Committee

IEEE Computer Society Distinguished Contributor,

(Inaugural Class)

Chair – Public Relations & Publication Standing Committee,

IEEE Delhi Section

of Practice, Chitkara University

BCI's C&R Business Continuity Manager of the Year Award India 2009

BCI's Merit Award Global 2012

BCI's Continuity & Resilience Contributor Award Middle East 2020

(and Global Finalist)

DRII's Lifetime Achievement Award 2021, 2022, 2024 (Finalist)

BCI's Continuity & Resilience Contributor Award Global, India & South Asia 2021

BCI's Hall of Fame

ILA's Global Outstanding Leadership Award 2021

Qualified Independent Director

(Ministry of Corporate Affairs, Govt. of India scheme)

Certified International Trainer, Certified Corporate Trainer, Mentor, Coach, Guide

15500+ hours Training/ Teaching|| Speaker|| Author|| Researcher|| Auditor|| Assessor|| 100% NPS||

ISO 22301/ NCEMA 7000|| ISO 31000|| ISO 22361|| ISO 22316||

Organisational Resilience|| BCM|| Crisis Management|| Enterprise Risk Management||

Operational Risk Management|| Operational Resilience|| Cybersecurity|| LinkedIn Invited Contributor||

LinkedIn Training and Development (HR) Top Voice|| 9 books|| 17 copyrights|| Udemy Instructor (3 courses)

Dedicated to Global Resilience (personal, professional Business, IT, Finance, Operational, Organisational, IT,.....). And to my family (My Organisational Resilience journey would not be complete and successful without their support).

Special thanks to my wife Bhavna who has always been a great support and helped in editing this book.

Anchita Sood deserves thanks and appreciation for editing the book with very tight schedules.

This one is for Planet Earth – a Resilient one!

A Note to Readers

This work is prohibited to be used as Creative Commons or with acknowledgement. Hence, you are requested to kindly refrain from illegal practices involving reproduction, copy, forward, disclose, publish, sale, display, trade or use any part of the copyright protected work. Otherwise, you will attract penal provisions of legal proceedings.

Preface

This book has been written by Daman Dev Sood.

The book on Third Party Ris Management, is perhaps, the only one of its type in content. Some chapters that have perhaps never been touched on any platform e.g. Materiality Assessment, Substitutivity Assessment, Manual Workarounds etc. I have developed multiple cases and case studies to explain the concepts. At the same time at least 4 new processes have been written to make TPRM easy, sensible, and practical.

This is in line with making the world a Resilient one!

Contents

FOREWORD-1 6

FOREWORD-2 8

Chapter 1: How To Read This Book 10

Chapter 2: Introduction...............................11

Chapter 3: Understanding Third Party Risks13

Chapter 4: Frameworks and Standards 15

Chapter 5. Developing a TPRM Program...31

Chapter 6: Integrating TPRM with Enterprise Risk Management (ERM)   44

Chapter 7: Due Diligence and Onboarding47

Chapter 8: Contracts and Service Level Agreements (SLAs)   56

Chapter 9: Ongoing Monitoring and Assessment   59

Chapter 10: Key Performance Indicators (KPIs) for Third Parties   61

Chapter 11: The TPRM Cycle 70

Chapter 12: Materiality Assessment and Substitutivity Assessment 73

Chapter 13: Vendor Selection Tips.............86

Chapter 14: The Role of AI in Third Party Risk Management   90

The Last Chapter: Responsible Sourcing ...93

One More Chapter: Technology Failures – Manual Workarounds   98

Guest Chapter 1: The Resilient Indian Economy in Light of Payment Digitisation 121

Guest Chapter 2: Lessons in Third-Party Risk Management from the Indus Valley Civilization   133

Guest Chapter 3: An Old Case of Third-Party Risk Management   136

Sample TPRMF, Third Party Policy, and Third Party Strategy   138

Case Studies in TPRM Implementation ...146

What is next for me?.. 163

FOREWORD-1

Zera Zheng

Global Head of Business Resilience Consulting, Maersk

September 2024

In the fast-evolving world of business, third-party risk management (TPRM) has become essential for resilience, regulatory compliance, and operational success. Professor Daman Sood's book, "My Experiment with Third Party Risk Management", offers a comprehensive, hands-on guide that addresses the "why," "what," and "how" of managing third-party risks.

Drawing on his deep expertise in various sectors, especially IT and finance, Professor Sood provides clear, actionable advice on navigating the complexities of TPRM. Whether you're tasked with designing a risk management program from scratch or refining an existing strategy, this book will serve as an indispensable resource. One of its standout features is the practical examples of communication strategies, which readers can adapt with minimal adjustments to fit their own organizational context.

I am honoured to have been invited by Professor Daman Sood to write the foreword for his remarkable book. Having had the privilege of working alongside him as part of the Program Advisory Group for the BCI 2024 Annual Event, I have witnessed firsthand his profound expertise and unwavering dedication to advancing risk management practices. His deep understanding of third-party risk management, combined with his passion for sharing knowledge, is evident throughout this book. I am grateful for the opportunity to contribute to this important work and to support Professor Sood in his mission to enhance resilience and compliance across industries.

Key Areas Covered:

Step-by-step guidance on how to effectively manage third-party risks for greater resilience and compliance.

Detailed advice on critical aspects to focus on when implementing a third-party risk management program.

Real-world examples of communication, assessment forms, and practical checklists to streamline implementation.

Who Will Benefit from This Book:

This book is versatile and applicable to a wide range of professionals:

Designing a Third-Party Risk Management Program: Ideal if you are building or revamping a TPRM program.

Developing Training Programs: Useful for those creating educational materials on TPRM.

Seeking Practice Sharing & References: A rich source of industry best practices and case studies.

Setting Strategy for Supplier Selection: Offers guidance on developing sound strategies for third-party evaluation.

Investing in TPRM Technology: Insights on leveraging AI and other emerging technologies for more efficient risk management.

Easy to Use, Whether You're a Beginner or an Expert

This book is thoughtfully designed to be accessible to both newcomers and seasoned professionals in the field of TPRM. For beginners, it serves as a practical guidebook, laying out clear steps on how to build a robust TPRM program from the ground up. For veterans, it functions as a valuable reference, providing checklists and tools to audit and improve existing programs.

The book's structure is both straightforward and detailed, guiding you through each phase of third-party risk management. Real-life examples are highlighted throughout, offering hands-on guidance for beginners and serving as valuable references and inspiration for veterans.

Chapter 5: Explores how to set objectives for your TPRM program, providing examples of potential objectives.

Chapter 7: Includes practical assessment forms for evaluating third-party vendors.

Chapter 8: Offers examples of Service Level Agreement (SLA) targets related to resilience that can be stipulated in contracts with third-party vendors.

Chapter 9: Shares ideas for key performance indicators (KPIs) that can be used to measure third-party performance in terms of resilience.

Chapter 12: Introduces a maturity assessment framework that evaluates suppliers based on criteria such as capacity, service reliability, lead time, and cost.

Chapter 13: Delves into how AI can enhance TPRM efforts and improve overall effectiveness.

Additionally, Professor Sood includes an insightful chapter on how to address potential disruptions from technology failures, like those related to CrowdStrike, and offers manual workarounds to ensure business continuity.

A Lasting Resource

After finishing this book, you'll feel as if you've completed an in-depth training course on TPRM, with the added advantage that you can always revisit and refer to it at any time. It's not just a book—it's an ongoing resource for your professional journey in third-party risk management.

FOREWORD-2

Andrew N. Hiles, Founder of the Business Continuity Institute, Professor Emeritus of BCM at Shanghai University's Telfort Business institute,

Author of How to Create & Maintain a Resilient Supply Chain www.rothstein.com

Past expert, Institute of Supply Chain Management

'My Experiments with BCM', Daman Dev Sood's last book opened new dimensions on the process of Impact Analysis, introducing readers to the concepts of emotional and social impacts.

It reminded me of my own thoughts on the shortcomings of traditional BIA: that they were all focused on short-term impacts of events an ignored the long-term context.

Examples:

Now, after two world wars, in which the immediate aftermath left UK and Germany weak and highly indebted, both winners and losers have recovered. Indeed, main the losers, Germany and Japan are now arguably the most influential countries with the biggest GDP in their zones while France, defeated, is also rich and highly influential.

Othe examples of BIA timeframe include:

BP Deepwater horizon oil spill, which caused the value of BP to crash from April 20, 2010,

But BP has recovered its value and remains a 'must have' in big investment portfolios.

Perrier mineral water, contaminated by benzine.

Perrier's green bottles disappeared for years, and Perrier was bought by Nestlé.

Perrier now has the support from one of the world's biggest food and beverage firms, with much greater security than its previous family owners could provide.

In this new book, Third party Risk Management, (TPRM) Daman Dev Sood again brings his vision and fresh insights to a key area of resilience and continuity.

Risk management processes have long been codified and mummified.

TPRM is usually focused on suppliers.

Even so, in over 40 years a consultant and practitioner of BCM, I have never known an organisation drill through its supply chain to see if there is a single point of failure in sub-suppliers. There often is

It may be dependence on an ISP, energy company, a government's tax regime, subject to change at short, or no notice. As this insightful and informative book shows, third parties can include any stakeholder in an entity, including regulators, trade unions, those who fund the entity, the media, government and customers.

Few organizations, even those practising Enterprise Risk Management, have identified all these risks or formulated and exercised plans to deal with such risks if they happen.

In this highly readable, insightful book, Daman Dev Sood reveals crucial but overlooked aspects of TPRM.

It should be essential reading for all involved in procurement, SCM, resilience, security and BCM.

Chapter 1: How To Read This Book

I have not deviated from my core i.e., Resilience. If the book makes you a better Consultant or Management Consultant, or Risk Manager it ultimately makes you Resilient. And **Resilient People Make Resilient Organisations!**

As an experiment, I have used AI to high level in authoring this book and have then extensively edited and refined to make it meaningful.

Enjoy the reading.

And I look forward to your views and feedback.

Chapter 2: Introduction

Overview of Third Party Risk Management (TPRM)

Definition and Importance

Third Party Risk Management (TPRM) involves the identification, assessment, and control of risks that arise from the organization's relationship with external entities. These entities include vendors, suppliers, service providers, partners, contractors, and any other third parties. Effective TPRM ensures that these relationships do not introduce unacceptable levels of risk to the organization.

Historical Context and Evolution

The concept of TPRM has evolved significantly over the past few decades. Initially, organizations primarily focused on internal risks. However, as globalization and outsourcing increased, the complexities of managing external entities became apparent. Significant incidents, such as the Target data breach in 2013, where an HVAC vendor was compromised, leading to massive data theft, highlighted the need for robust TPRM frameworks.

In November and December of 2013, Target Corporation suffered one of the largest cyber breaches to date. The breach that occurred during the busy holiday shopping season resulted in personal and credit card information of approximately 110 million Target customers being compromised. The case describes the details of the breach, circumstances that lead to it, consequences for customers and for Target, and the company's response. Additionally, the case discusses the role of management and the board of directors in cyber security at Target. Target's board of directors was subject to intense criticism by shareholders and governance experts such as the leading proxy advisor Institutional Shareholder Services (ISS). Lastly, the case discusses the critique and defense of the board's role and is designed to allow for a discussion of the causes and consequences of the cyber breach and accountability of directors in cyber security.[1]

Benefits of Managing Third-Party Risks

1. Enhanced Operational Resilience

- **Continuous Operations**: Effective third-party risk management ensures that critical services provided by third parties remain uninterrupted.
- **Supply Chain Stability**: Identifying and mitigating risks within the supply chain prevents disruptions, ensuring smooth production and delivery processes.

2. Financial Protection

- **Cost Avoidance**: By proactively managing third-party risks, organizations can avoid significant financial losses due to third-party failures, fraud, or breaches.
- **Improved Budget Management**: Understanding and mitigating risks helps in better forecasting and allocation of resources.

3. Regulatory Compliance

- **Avoidance of Fines and Penalties**: Effective risk management ensures compliance with laws and regulations, reducing the risk of legal penalties and fines.
- **Enhanced Reporting**: Comprehensive risk management processes aid in accurate and timely reporting to regulatory bodies.

---

[1] Suraj Srinivasan, Lynn S. Paine and Neeraj Goyal, Cyber Breach at Target, Harvard Business School July 2016 available at - https://www.hbs.edu/faculty/Pages/item.aspx?num=51339

4. Reputation and Brand Protection

- **Trust and Credibility**: Proactively managing risks associated with third parties helps maintain and enhance the organization's reputation among customers, investors, and other stakeholders.
- **Crisis Management**: Preparedness and effective response to third-party incidents can mitigate negative publicity and protect the brand.

5. Improved Strategic Decision-Making

- **Informed Decisions**: Comprehensive risk assessments provide insights that support strategic decision-making and planning.
- **Competitive Advantage**: Organizations that manage third-party risks effectively can leverage their robust risk management practices as a differentiator in the market.

6. Enhanced Security and Data Protection

- **Data Integrity**: Ensuring third parties adhere to security protocols helps protect sensitive information from breaches.
- **Cybersecurity**: Mitigating cybersecurity risks associated with third parties reduces the likelihood of cyber-attacks and data breaches.

7. Stronger Relationships with Third Parties

- **Better Collaboration**: Clear risk management expectations and processes foster stronger, more transparent relationships with third parties.
- **Performance Monitoring**: Continuous monitoring and evaluation of third-party performance lead to better service delivery and value.

8. Risk Mitigation and Contingency Planning

- **Early Detection**: Identifying potential risks at early stage enables organizations to implement mitigation strategies promptly.
- **Contingency Plans**: Having well-defined contingency plans in place helps manage and recover from third-party failures more efficiently.

9. Sustainability and Corporate Responsibility

- **Ethical Practices**: Ensuring third parties comply with ethical standards and practices supports the organization's corporate social responsibility (CSR) goals.
- **Sustainable Sourcing**: Managing risks associated with sourcing and procurement helps in promoting sustainability within the supply chain.

Conclusion

Managing third-party risks is essential for organizations to ensure operational continuity, financial stability, regulatory compliance, and reputation protection. By adopting effective third-party risk management practices, organizations can build resilience, foster stronger relationships with third parties, and achieve strategic objectives, ultimately leading to sustained success and growth.

Chapter 3: Understanding Third Party Risks

1. Types of Third Party Risks

Operational Risk

Operational risk involves failures in the day-to-day operations caused by third parties. This can include disruptions due to natural disasters, human error, or technical failures. For example, if a key supplier fails to deliver critical components on time, it can halt production and lead to significant financial losses.

Compliance Risk

Compliance risk arises when third parties fail to comply with laws, regulations, or internal policies. This can result in legal penalties, financial losses, and reputational damage. An example is a vendor not adhering to data protection regulations, such as GDPR, leading to hefty fines for the contracting organization.

Financial Risk

Financial risk pertains to the financial stability of third parties. A vendor's bankruptcy can disrupt supply chains and affect the organization's operations. For instance, during the COVID-19 pandemic, many businesses faced financial instability, affecting their ability to fulfill contractual obligations.

Strategic Risk

Strategic risk occurs when a third party's business strategies or actions conflict with the organization's strategic goals. For example, if a strategic partner enters a competing market, it could undermine the organization's market position and strategic initiatives.

Reputational Risk

Reputational risk arises when a third party's actions negatively impact the organization's reputation. For instance, if a supplier is found to be using unethical labor practices, it can lead to public backlash and damage the organization's brand.

Cybersecurity Risk

Cybersecurity risk involves threats to information security, such as data breaches, ransomware attacks, or system compromises originating from third parties. An example is a cloud service provider being breached, exposing sensitive data of the organization.

Environmental, Social, and Governance (ESG) Risk

ESG risk encompasses the environmental impact, social responsibility, and governance practices of third parties. For example, a supplier's poor environmental practices can lead to regulatory fines and damage the organization's sustainability commitments.

Basically, whatever can happen to your organization, can happen to your third parties too!

2. Identifying Third Parties

Categories of Third Parties

- **Vendors:** Providers of goods and services critical to operations
- **Suppliers:** Entities that supply raw materials or components for production

- **Partners:** Business allies in joint ventures or strategic alliances
- **Contractors:** Independent professionals or firms contracted for specific tasks
- **Service Providers:** Entities offering specialized services such as IT, legal, or consulting.

RBI (Reserve Bank of India) in its 'Guidance Note on Operational Risk Management and Operational Resilience' has given an example as shown below :-

Examples of Third Paty Service Providers			
Direct Selling Agents	Cash/ ATM Management Company	IT/ OT Vendors	Customer Care Services Providers
External Consultants	Advertising Partners	Recovery Agencies	Analytics Services Providers
Storage/ Backup Providers	Payment Processing Firms	Cloud Services Providers	Logistics Services Providers
Marketing Agents	Legal Services Providers	Data Management Companies	

3. Mapping and Inventory of Third Parties

Creating a comprehensive inventory of all third parties is essential for managing third-party risks. This involves:

- Listing all third parties and their contact details
- Categorizing them based on their role and importance to the organization
- Maintaining updated records of contracts, agreements, and performance metrics

4. Risk Segmentation and Prioritization

Not all third parties pose the same level of risk. It is crucial that an organization segments and prioritizes third parties based on factors such as:

- **Criticality:** How essential the third party is to core operations
- **Data Access:** The level of access the third party has to sensitive information
- **Historical Performance:** The third party's track record of reliability and compliance
- **Geographical Location:** Risks associated with operating in different regions

Chapter 4: Frameworks and Standards

1. Regulatory Landscape

Overview of Relevant Regulations

TPRM is influenced by a variety of regulations depending on the industry and geographical location. Some key regulations include:

1.1 General Data Protection Regulation (GDPR): Protects data privacy in the EU.

I found it very difficult to understand GDPR, hence I am not able to write much. But simply put, it's about data privacy, so third parties who have your customers' data, should also follow the requirements of GDPR.

1.2 California Consumer Privacy Act (CCPA): Enhances privacy rights for residents of California.

1.3 California Privacy Rights Act (CPRA):

These two being a state specific, I will discuss at the end of this chapter.

1.4 Sarbanes-Oxley Act (SOX): Mandates strict reforms to improve financial disclosures and prevent accounting fraud in the US.

The SOX Act, enacted in 2002, was designed to improve corporate governance and financial transparency in response to major corporate scandals. It has specific requirements that impact TPRM in several ways:

1. **Internal Controls and Audits:**
   o SOX requires companies to establish and maintain an adequate internal control structure and procedures for financial reporting (Section 404). Companies must ensure that third parties, such as vendors and service providers, adhere to these controls when handling financial data.
2. **Vendor Management:**
   o Companies must perform due diligence on their third-party vendors to ensure they have adequate controls in place. This includes assessing the financial stability, control environment, and compliance history of these vendors.
3. **Compliance and Reporting:**
   o Under SOX, companies are required to report on their internal controls over financial reporting. This includes controls related to third-party activities. Companies must ensure that third parties comply with relevant regulations and contractual obligations, which is a key aspect of TPRM.
4. **Risk Assessments:**
   o SOX emphasizes the need for ongoing risk assessments, including risks posed by third parties. Companies need to identify, assess, and mitigate risks associated with their third-party relationships to ensure compliance with SOX requirements.
5. **Documentation and Evidence:**
   o SOX compliance requires thorough documentation of internal controls and procedures, including those involving third parties. Companies must maintain evidence of their TPRM activities, such as vendor assessments, contracts, and monitoring reports.

1.5 Health Insurance Portability and Accountability Act (HIPAA): Protects sensitive patient health information in the US.

The Health Insurance Portability and Accountability Act (HIPAA) is closely related to Third Party Risk Management (TPRM) in the healthcare industry. HIPAA establishes national standards to protect sensitive patient health information from being disclosed without the patient's consent or knowledge. It has several provisions that impact TPRM:

1. **Business Associate Agreements (BAAs):**
   - o Covered entities (such as healthcare providers, health plans, and healthcare clearinghouses) must have written contracts, known as Business Associate Agreements, with their third-party service providers (business associates). These agreements outline the responsibilities of the business associates to protect the privacy and security of Protected Health Information (PHI).
2. **Due Diligence:**
   - o Covered entities must perform due diligence on their business associates to ensure they have adequate safeguards in place to protect PHI. This includes assessing the business associate's security measures, compliance with HIPAA regulations, and overall ability to manage PHI securely.
3. **Risk Assessments:**
   - o Covered entities and their business associates should conduct regular risk assessments to identify potential vulnerabilities and threats to PHI. This includes evaluating the risks posed by third parties who handle or have access to PHI.
4. **Training and Awareness:**
   - o Covered entities must ensure that their business associates are properly trained in HIPAA requirements and understand their responsibilities for protecting PHI. This includes ongoing education and awareness programs related to data privacy and security.
5. **Breach Notification:**
   - o Business associates should notify covered entities of any breach of unsecured PHI. This requires having processes in place to detect, respond to, and report breaches involving third parties in a timely manner.
6. **Compliance Monitoring:**
   - o Covered entities must monitor their business associates to ensure ongoing compliance with HIPAA requirements. This can involve regular audits, reviews, and assessments of the business associates' practices and procedures for handling PHI.

1.6 Operational Resilience – there is a lot happening in this space, specifically in the Financial Industry so I will have a lengthy discussion later in this chapter.

1.7 Industry-Specific Guidelines

Different industries have specific guidelines to manage third-party risks:

- **Financial Services:** a lot has been covered in Operational Resilience below
- **Healthcare:** HIPAA, HITECH Act.

I have covered HIPPA earlier.

The Health Information Technology for Economic and Clinical Health (HITECH) Act, enacted in 2009, is designed to promote the adoption and meaningful use of health information technology. HITECH is closely related to Third Party Risk Management (TPRM) in the healthcare industry, particularly concerning the handling of Protected Health Information (PHI).

1. **Enhanced HIPAA Enforcement:**
   - o HITECH strengthens the enforcement of HIPAA regulations, including increasing penalties for non-compliance. This heightened enforcement necessitates robust TPRM practices to ensure that third parties handling PHI are compliant with HIPAA and HITECH requirements.
2. **Breach Notification Requirements:**
   - o HITECH imposes stricter breach notification requirements for PHI. Both covered entities and their business associates must notify affected individuals, the Department of Health and Human Services (HHS), and sometimes the media, in the event of a data breach. Effective TPRM involves ensuring that third parties have processes in place for timely breach detection and notification.
3. **Extension of HIPAA Obligations to Business Associates:**
   - o Under HITECH, business associates of covered entities are directly subject to HIPAA regulations. This means third parties that handle PHI must implement the same safeguards as covered entities. TPRM must include verifying that business associates are compliant with these extended obligations.
4. **Meaningful Use and EHR Adoption:**
   - o HITECH encourages the adoption of Electronic Health Records (EHR) systems through financial incentives. Ensuring that EHR vendors and other third parties comply with privacy and security

standards is a critical aspect of TPRM. This includes evaluating the security measures and compliance status of EHR providers.

5. **Increased Accountability:**
   o HITECH increases the accountability of both covered entities and business associates by requiring audits and investigations. TPRM processes should include regular audits and assessments of third-party compliance with HITECH and HIPAA standards to avoid penalties.
6. **Security Provisions:**
   o HITECH mandates that business associates implement administrative, physical, and technical safeguards to protect PHI. TPRM involves assessing these safeguards during the vendor selection process and continuously monitoring third-party compliance.

1.8 Technology: NIST Cybersecurity Framework

The NIST Cybersecurity Framework (NIST CSF) provides guidelines for organizations to manage and reduce cybersecurity risk. It is widely used across various industries to enhance cybersecurity practices, and it includes specific considerations for Third Party Risk Management (TPRM).

1. **Identify Function:**
   o **Asset Management:** Organizations should manage asset inventories, including those owned by third parties, to ensure all assets are accounted for and protected.
   o **Supply Chain Risk Management:** This category focuses on identifying and assessing cybersecurity risks within the supply chain. It involves understanding the third-party ecosystem, including suppliers and service providers, and assessing their risk posture.
2. **Protect Function:**
   o **Access Control:** Organizations must ensure that third parties have appropriate access controls in place to protect sensitive information and systems.
   o **Awareness and Training:** Third parties should receive appropriate training on cybersecurity policies and procedures to ensure they understand their roles and responsibilities.
   o **Data Security:** Data security measures should extend to third parties, ensuring they handle and protect data according to the organization's standards.
   o **Protective Technology:** Ensure that third parties use appropriate technologies and processes to protect against cybersecurity threats.
3. **Detect Function:**
   o **Security Continuous Monitoring:** Organizations should continuously monitor third-party activities to detect potential cybersecurity incidents and ensure ongoing compliance with security requirements.
   o **Detection Processes:** Establish and maintain detection processes that include third-party activities and services.
4. **Respond Function:**
   o **Response Planning:** Develop and implement response plans that include procedures for dealing with cybersecurity incidents involving third parties.
   o **Communications:** Ensure effective communication with third parties during and after a cybersecurity incident to coordinate response efforts.
5. **Recover Function:**
   o **Recovery Planning:** Include third parties in recovery planning to ensure they can support the organization's recovery efforts after a cybersecurity incident.
   o **Improvements:** Continuously improve recovery strategies by incorporating lessons learned from incidents involving third parties.

Specific TPRM Considerations in NIST CSF:

- **Third-Party Risk Assessments:**
  o Conduct regular risk assessments of third parties to identify and evaluate potential cybersecurity risks they may pose to the organization.
- **Third-Party Security Requirements:**
  o Establish security requirements for third parties and incorporate these into contracts and agreements to ensure they comply with the organization's cybersecurity policies.
- **Third-Party Monitoring and Auditing:**
  o Implement processes for ongoing monitoring and auditing of third-party security practices to ensure continuous compliance and identify any emerging risks.
- **Incident Response and Recovery with Third Parties:**

o   Develop coordinated incident response and recovery plans that include third-party roles and responsibilities to ensure a unified approach to managing and mitigating cybersecurity incidents.

1.9 Operational Resilience

Basel Committee on Banking Supervision (BCBS)

Through its 'Basel Principles for Operational Resilience d516', the committee has emphasized on need of TPRM. There are multiple references to managing third parties throughout the document. Principle 5 (Third-party dependency management) is specifically devoted to TPRM.

It is worth noting that the document specifies *"Banks should manage their dependencies on relationships, including those of, but not limited to, third parties or intragroup entities, for the delivery of critical operations."*

Further BCBS guidance on outsourcing of services can be found in documents published through the Joint Forum (BCBS- IOSCO-IAIS), *Outsourcing in financial services*, February 2005.[2]

The management of dependencies articulated in this principle should be consistent with and conducted alongside the control and risk mitigation policies as articulated in paragraph 51 of Principle 9 in the PSMOR.

Banks should perform a risk assessment and due diligence before entering into arrangements including those of, but not limited to, third parties or intragroup entities, consistent with the bank's operational risk management framework, outsourcing/third-party risk management policy and operational resilience approach. Prior to the bank entering into such an arrangement, the bank should verify whether the third party, including, if relevant, the intragroup entity to these arrangements, has at least equivalent level of operational resilience to safeguard the bank's critical operations in both normal circumstances and in the event of disruption.

Banks should develop appropriate business continuity and contingency planning procedures and exit strategies to maintain their operational resilience in the event of a failure or disruption at a third party impacting the provision of critical operations. Scenarios under the bank's business continuity plans should assess the substitutability of third parties that provide services to the bank's critical operations, and other viable alternatives that may facilitate operational resilience in the event of an outage at a third party, such as bringing the service back in-house."

Federal Reserve System

Through its guidance document 'FRB bcreg20201030a1', FRS puts importance to TPRM with multiple references throughout and Chapter 4 (Third-Party Risk Management) specifically going deep in expectations as:

"

a) The firm identifies and analyzes third-party risk of critical operations and core business lines. It prioritizes third-party dependencies that are most significant to the firm and understands, manages, and mitigates its risks.

b) The firm establishes relationships with third parties through formal agreements. The firm manages and monitors the performance of third parties against its service requirements and its tolerance for disruption.

c) The firm periodically reviews reports of systems and controls and summaries of test results or other equivalent assessments of third parties. It establishes processes and benchmarks for monitoring a third party's ability to continue to deliver services during disruptions.

d) The firm verifies that third parties have sound risk management practices and controls in place that serve to identify and mitigate hazards to operations and are consistent with the firm's tolerance for disruption.

e) The firm addresses key third-party concerns to the extent that these concerns affect the firm's operational resilience (e.g., through due diligence, contract negotiations, ongoing monitoring, and termination of contracts).

f) The firm identifies risks of third parties that provide it with public and critical infrastructure services, such as energy and telecommunications. The firm has processes to manage disruptions of these services and updates these processes as appropriate to stay within its tolerance for disruption.

g) The firm identifies other third parties that may be available to assist in the event its current third parties are unable to continue delivering services. The firm assesses the substitutability of third parties that provide services

---

[2] www.bis.org/publ/joint12.pdf

supporting the firm's critical operations and core business lines including the possibility of bringing a service back in-house. "

DORA (Digital Operational Resilience Act)

Mainly targeted at the Financial sector of the EU and focuses on ICT only. It is a regulation. I found it easier to understand this compared with the GDPR. The regulation is full of references to third parties. Chapter V is fully devoted to TPRM (Managing of ICT Third-Party Risk).

Here are the key aspects related to Third-Party Risk Management (TPRM) under DORA:

1. **Scope and Applicability**: DORA applies to a wide range of financial entities, including banks, investment firms, insurance companies, and other financial market infrastructures. It also extends to critical third-party service providers that provide ICT-related services to these entities.
2. **Risk Management Framework**: Financial entities must establish a comprehensive risk management framework that includes policies, procedures, and controls for managing ICT risk. This framework should cover the entire lifecycle of third-party relationships, from selection to termination.
3. **Due Diligence and Monitoring**: DORA requires financial entities to conduct thorough due diligence before engaging third-party ICT service providers. This involves assessing the provider's ability to manage and mitigate ICT risks. Continuous monitoring of third-party performance and risk is also mandated to ensure ongoing compliance.
4. **Contractual Arrangements**: Financial entities must have written contracts with third-party ICT service providers. These contracts should include clear provisions on ICT security, data protection, and incident management. They must also specify the rights and obligations of both parties, including termination conditions.
5. **Concentration Risk**: DORA emphasizes the need to identify and manage concentration risks arising from over-reliance on a single or a few third-party providers. Financial entities should diversify their third-party relationships to avoid significant disruptions in case of a provider's failure.
6. **Incident Reporting**: Third-party ICT service providers must have robust incident management processes in place. They are required to report significant ICT-related incidents to their financial entity clients without undue delay. Financial entities, in turn, must report these incidents to the relevant authorities.
7. **Testing and Audits**: Regular testing of third-party ICT service providers' systems and controls is required to ensure they meet the security and resilience standards. Financial entities should also conduct audits or request third-party audit reports to verify compliance.
8. **Supervisory Oversight**: DORA grants regulatory authorities the power to oversee and supervise critical third-party ICT service providers. These providers may be required to register with the authorities and undergo regular assessments to ensure they adhere to the required standards.
9. **Business Continuity and Disaster Recovery**: Financial entities and their third-party ICT service providers must have robust business continuity and disaster recovery plans. These plans should ensure the continuity of critical functions in the event of a disruption and be regularly tested and updated.
10. **Information Sharing**: DORA encourages information sharing between financial entities, third-party providers, and regulatory authorities to enhance overall operational resilience. This includes sharing information on threats, vulnerabilities, and incidents.

Bank of England's Operational Resilience Policy

The base document 'Bank of England operational-resilience-march-2021' clearly mentions "

As set out in the PRA's outsourcing rules, firms remain responsible for their obligations when functions are outsourced to a third party. In the PRA's operational resilience policy, the PRA expects firms to be operationally resilient regardless of any outsourcing arrangements or use of third parties. Firms should not allow their ability to deliver their important business services within their impact tolerances to be undermined when they are delivered wholly or in part by third parties, whether these third parties are other entities within their group or external providers.

The PRA's policy for modernising the regulatory framework on outsourcing and third party risk management (SS2/21 'Outsourcing and third party risk management') complements the PRA's operational resilience policy. SS2/21 reflects the increased importance to firms of cloud computing and other new technologies. The PRA's approach is to consider SS2/21 and the PRA's operational resilience policy in combination."

The associated document "Bank of England ss221-march-21" is fully dedicated to TPRM and is named "Outsourcing and third party risk management". A quick look at the summary (adopted from the document itself) helps to understand the depth of coverage:

"

Chapter 2 elaborates on the definition of 'outsourcing' in the PRA Rulebook. It also notes that there are arrangements between firms and third parties that fall outside this definition ('third party arrangements') and are consequently outside of the scope of existing requirements on outsourcing and some of the detailed expectations in this SS. However, these third party arrangements are still subject to the PRA Fundamental Rules and other PRA requirements and expectations on business continuity, governance, operational resilience, and risk management (including but not limited to cyber risk).

Chapter 3 clarifies how the principle of proportionality applies to the expectations in this SS. In particular, to intragroup outsourcing and to 'non-significant firms' (as defined in paragraph 3.9 of this SS).

Chapter 4 sets out the PRA's expectations on governance, including under the Senior Managers and Certification Regime (SM&CR), and record keeping.

Chapter 5 sets out the PRA's expectations for firms during the pre-outsourcing phase. It addresses the materiality and risk assessments of their outsourcing and other third party arrangements (including notification to the PRA where required), and firms' due diligence on third parties.

Chapter 6 lists the areas that the PRA expects written agreements relating to material outsourcing to address as a minimum. The following four areas are then examined in detail in Chapters 7–10:

- data security (Chapter 7);

- access, audit, and information rights (Chapter 8);

- sub-outsourcing (Chapter 9); and

- business continuity and exit strategies (Chapter 10)."

Central Bank of Ireland

Central bank of Ireland's "cross-industry-guidance-on-operational-resilience" also clearly sets the expectations "Operational resilience requires coordination between risk management, business continuity management (BCM), incident management, third party risk management, Information Communication Technology (ICT) and cyber risk, and recovery and resolution planning."
And
"As operational resilience draws from elements of business continuity, third party risk management, ICT & cyber risk management, incident management, and wider aspects of operational risk management, a holistic approach is essential if a firm is to enhance the resilience of its business services, regardless of the type of disruption."

In its 3 Pillars approach, the bank uses Guideline 8 to take care of third party risks as "Guideline 8: A firm should capture third party dependencies in the mapping of critical or important business services."

OPERATIONAL RESILIENCE

Pillar1: Identify & Prepare	Pillar2: Respond & Adapt	Pillar3: Recover & Learn
1. The Board has ultimate responsibility for the Operational Resilience of a firm. 2. The Operational Resilience Framework should be aligned with a firm's overall Governance and Risk Management Frameworks. 3. The Board reviews and approves the criteria for critical or important business services. 4. A firm should identify its critical or important business services. 5. Impact tolerances should be approved for each critical or important business service. 6. A firm should develop clear impact tolerance metrics. 7. A firm should understand and map out how its critical or important business services are delivered. 8. A firm should capture third party dependencies in the mapping of critical or important business services. 9. A firm should have ICT and Cyber Resilience strategies that are integral to the operational resilience of its critical or important business services. 10. A firm should document and test its ability to remain within impact tolerances through severe but plausible scenarios.	11. Business Continuity Management should be fully integrated into the overarching Operational Resilience Framework and linked to a firm's risk appetite. 12. The Incident Management Strategy should be fully integrated into the overarching Operational Resilience Framework. 13. Internal and External Crisis Communication plans should be fully integrated into the overarching Operational Resilience Framework	14. A lessons learned exercise should be conducted after a disruption to a critical or important business service to enhance a firm's capabilities to adapt and respond to future operational events. 15. A firm should promote an effective culture of learning and continuous improvement as operational resilience evolves.

Reserve Bank of India

Through its guidance note "RBI Guidance Note on Operational Risk Management and Operational Resilience" RBI also emphasized on the need of TPRM. Guideline 12 "Third-party dependency management" talks about this. Principle 11 says "Organisations should manage their dependencies on relationships, including those of, but not limited to, third parties (which include intragroup entities), for the delivery of critical operations. "

ORM & OR

Pillar1: Prepare & Protect	Pillar2: Build Resilience	Pillar3: Learn and Adapt
1. Governance and Risk Culture	7. Business Continuity Planning and Testing	12. Disclosure and Reporting
2. Responsibilities of Board of Directors and Senior Management	8. Mapping interconnections & Interdependencies	
3. Risk Management: Identification and Assessment	9. Third party dependency management	13. Lessons Learned Exercise and Adapting
4. Change Management		
5. Monitoring and Reporting	10. Incident management	
6. Control and Mitigation	11. ICT including cyber security	14. Continuous Improvement through Feedback Systems

In all guidelines, the expectation is to go to the 4th, 5th and 6th parties. The RBI guidance narrates this expectation as "Therefore, organisations, in their agreement with the service providers, should include clauses making the service provider contractually liable for the performance and risk management practices of its sub-contractors (including nth parties in the supply chain)."

Australian Prudential Regulation Authority (APRA)

Through its 'Prudential Standard CPS 230' (which surprisingly is dated July 2025 on the day i.e. 18/07/2024 when I am writing this chapter) is not so specific about TPRM but does mention effective management of Operational Risks and Business Continuity.

Hong Kong Monetary Authority (HKMA)

Through its 'Supervisory Policy Manual on Operational Resilience (OR2)' puts the requirements with respect to TPRM as "Third-party dependency management: As AIs increasingly engage third parties or intragroup entities for the provision of services or delivery of functions, they should endeavour to prevent disruptions at these entities from affecting critical operations delivery. To ensure potential risks to critical operations are minimised, AIs should manage their dependencies on third parties and intragroup entities as they would with outsourcing arrangements. Prior to entering into arrangements that support the delivery of critical operations, an AI should verify whether the relevant third parties or intragroup entities have at least equivalent level of operational resilience to that of the AI. Where such verification is not feasible, the AI should take alternative steps to satisfy itself that the engagement of the third party or intragroup entity would not weaken its ability to deliver critical operations in the event of a disruption. During the course of engagement, an AI should have adequate arrangements in place to continually satisfy itself that the third party or intragroup entity has maintained an acceptable level of operational resilience. In addition, an AI should develop appropriate business continuity and contingency planning procedures and exit strategies to maintain its operational resilience in the event of a failure or disruption at a third party or intragroup entity which may impact its delivery of critical operations. An AI should not enter into, or continue, any third party or intragroup arrangements that may weaken the operational resilience of the AI's critical operations."

Monetary Authority of Singapore (MAS)

MAS has not issued Operational Resilience guidelines or requirements separately, but within its 'BCM-Guidelines-June-2022' has defined the expectations in Chapter 4 as "Third-Party Dependencies 4.3 Many FIs engage third parties8 to support the delivery of their critical business services. These arrangements could increase operational risks arising from the failure, delay, or compromise of a third party in providing the service.

4.4 The FI should put in place measures that enable third parties to meet the SRTOs of its critical business services. This can be done through measures, such as the following:

a. establish and regularly review operational level or service level agreements with third parties that set out specific and measurable recovery expectations and support the FI's BCM;

b. review the BCPs of third parties and verify that the BCPs meet appropriate standards and are regularly tested;

c. establish arrangements with third parties to safeguard the availability of resources, such as requesting for dedicated manpower;

d. conduct audits on the third parties; or

e. perform joint tests with third parties.

4.5 The FI should also put in place plans and procedures10 to address any unforeseen disruption, failure or termination of third-party arrangements to minimize the impact of such adverse events on the continuity of its critical business services.

4.6 As far as possible, the FI should put in place measures to address the disruption of common utility services11 supporting critical business services, such as implementing redundancy or alternative contingency arrangements."

Dubai Financial Services Authority (DFSA)

Through its 'Rule Book for Authorised Market Institutions (AMI)', DFSA mentions in rule 5.5 'Operational efficiency and resilience 'that the dependencies on outsourcing need to be managed appropriately.

All above are national level guidelines/ acts/ regulations. It is interesting to note that California in the USA has two acts, the California Consumer Privacy Act (CCPA) and the California Privacy Rights Act (CPRA) that have impact on TPRM. So, I am treating them a little differently.

California Consumer Privacy Act (CCPA)

Key Provisions:

- **Consumer Rights:** Grants California residents the right to know what personal data is being collected about them, to whom it is being sold, and the ability to access, delete, and opt-out of the sale of their personal information.
- **Disclosure Requirements:** Organizations must disclose their data collection practices, the categories of personal data collected, and the purposes for which it is used.
- **Third-Party Contracts:** Organizations need to ensure that their contracts with third parties include provisions that require compliance with the CCPA, particularly regarding data use and consumer rights.

Impact on TPRM:

- **Due Diligence:** Organizations must perform due diligence to ensure that third parties handling personal data comply with CCPA requirements.
- **Contractual Obligations:** Contracts with third parties should include specific terms that mandate compliance with CCPA, including data protection measures and the handling of consumer rights requests.
- **Monitoring and Auditing:** Continuous monitoring and periodic audits of third parties are necessary to ensure ongoing compliance.

California Privacy Rights Act (CPRA)

Key Provisions:

- **Expanded Consumer Rights:** Enhances the rights provided under CCPA, including the right to correct inaccurate personal data and the right to limit the use of sensitive personal information.
- **Data Minimization:** Requires organizations to limit data collection to what is necessary for the disclosed purpose.
- **Automated Decision-Making:** Introduces regulations on the use of automated decision-making technologies.
- **Dedicated Enforcement Agency:** Establishes the California Privacy Protection Agency (CPPA) to enforce compliance.

Impact on TPRM:

- **Enhanced Due Diligence:** Organizations need to extend their due diligence to ensure third parties also comply with the expanded rights and data minimization principles under CPRA.
- **Updated Contracts:** Contracts with third parties must be updated to include compliance with CPRA requirements, especially concerning new consumer rights and data protection standards.
- **Vendor Assessments:** More comprehensive vendor assessments and audits are required to evaluate compliance with CPRA, particularly in areas such as automated decision-making and the handling of sensitive personal information.

Good Practices for TPRM Compliance with CCPA and CPRA

1. **Vendor Risk Assessments:** Conduct thorough risk assessments of third parties to evaluate their data protection practices and compliance with CCPA and CPRA.
2. **Contract Management:** Ensure that contracts with third parties include clauses that mandate compliance with CCPA and CPRA, including provisions for data protection, consumer rights, and audits.
3. **Ongoing Monitoring:** Implement continuous monitoring and regular audits of third parties to ensure ongoing compliance with privacy regulations.
4. **Training and Awareness:** Provide training to third parties on the requirements of CCPA and CPRA and ensure they are aware of their obligations.
5. **Incident Response:** Establish clear protocols for incident response and data breach notification involving third parties, in line with CCPA and CPRA requirements.

The above Good Practices will generally be good for all regulations/ acts/ guidelines.

2. Risk Management Frameworks

ISO 31000

ISO 31000 provides guidelines on managing risk faced by organizations. It can be used by any organization regardless of its size, industry, or sector. Key elements include:

- **Risk Assessment:** Identifying, analyzing, and evaluating risks.
- **Risk Treatment:** Selecting and implementing measures to mitigate risks.
- **Monitoring and Review:** Continuously monitoring risk management processes.

The following text from the standard is highly valuable:

"This document is for use by people who create and protect value in organizations by managing risks, making decisions, setting and achieving objectives and improving performance.

Organizations of all types and sizes face external and internal factors and influences that make it uncertain whether they will achieve their objectives.

Managing risk is iterative and assists organizations in setting strategy, achieving objectives and making informed decisions.

Managing risk is part of governance and leadership and is fundamental to how the organization is managed at all levels. It contributes to the improvement of management systems.

Managing risk is part of all activities associated with an organization and includes interaction with stakeholders.

Managing risk considers the external and internal context of the organization, including human behaviour and cultural factors."

The following picture shows the three components of the standard i.e. Principles. Framework, and Process.

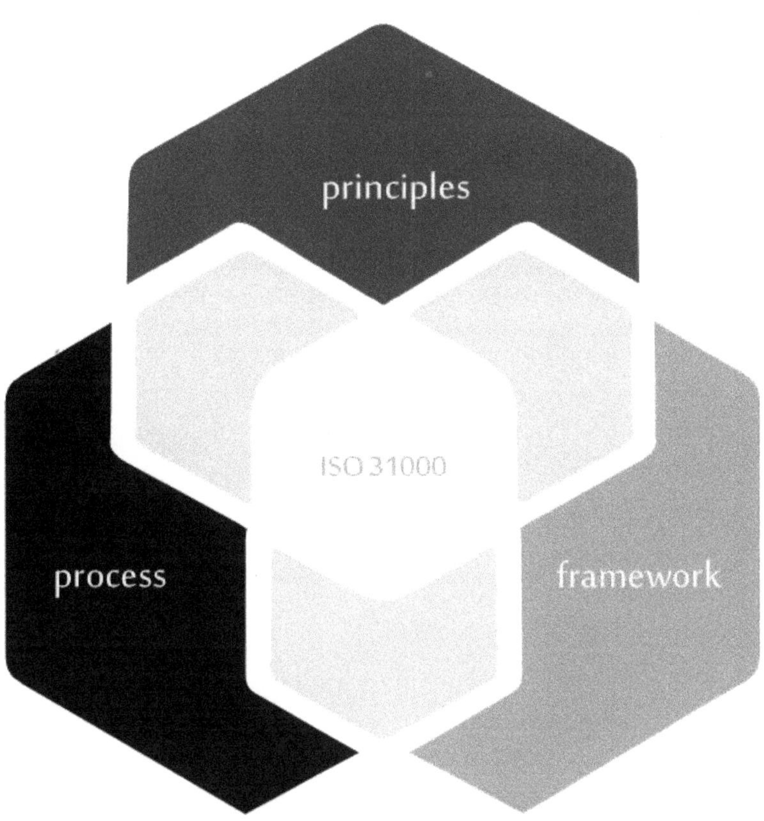

The following diagram helps to understand ISO 31000 in a gist – how principles, process, and framework are interlinked. By following this, an organization will be able to establish an RMS (Risk Management System) which can be used for TPRM as well.

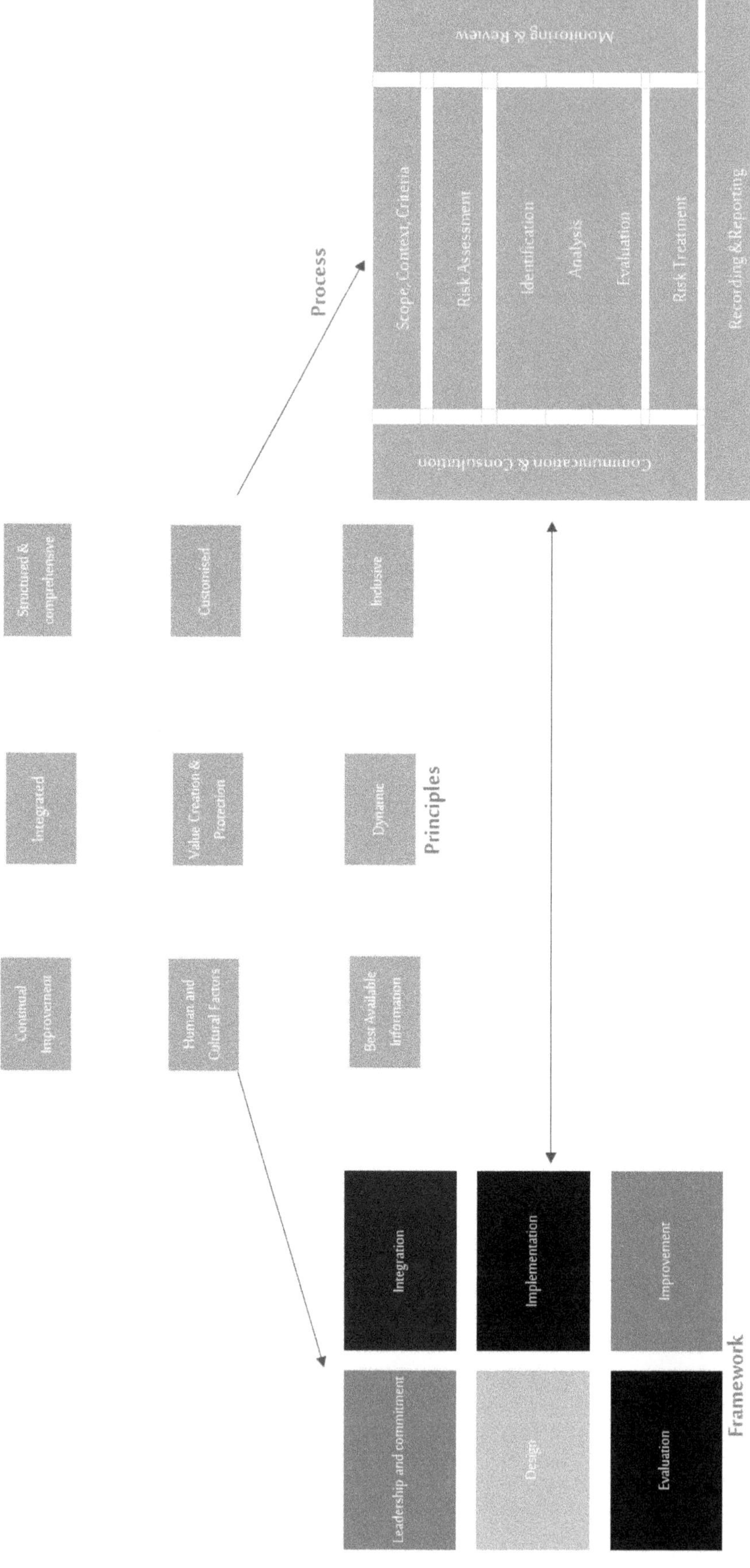

Process
Scope, Context, Criteria
Risk Assessment
Identification
Analysis
Evaluation
Risk Treatment
Monitoring & Review
Communication & Consultation
Recording & Reporting
Structured & comprehensive
Customised
Inclusive
Integrated
Value Creation & Protection
Dynamic
Continual Improvement
Human and Cultural Factors
Best Available Information
Principles
Integration
Implementation
Improvement
Leadership and commitment
Design
Evaluation
Framework

COSO Framework

The COSO framework provides a model for evaluating internal controls. It helps organizations:

- Establish risk management objectives.
- Identify and assess risks.
- Implement and monitor risk mitigation strategies.

NIST Cybersecurity Framework

The NIST Cybersecurity Framework provides a policy framework of computer security guidance for how private sector organizations in the US can assess and improve their ability to prevent, detect, and respond to cyber-attacks. Key components include:

- **Identify:** Develop an organizational understanding to manage cybersecurity risk.
- **Protect:** Develop and implement appropriate safeguards.
- **Detect:** Develop and implement appropriate activities to identify cybersecurity events.
- **Respond:** Develop and implement appropriate activities to take action regarding a detected cybersecurity event.
- **Recover:** Develop and implement appropriate activities to maintain plans for resilience and to restore capabilities.

ISO 22301

ISO 22301:2019 (Security and resilience — Business continuity management systems — Requirements) is the standard for business continuity. The following text from the standard is important:

"A BCMS emphasizes the importance of:

- understanding the organization's needs and the necessity for establishing business continuity policies and objectives;
- operating and maintaining processes, capabilities and response structures for ensuring the organization will survive disruptions;
- monitoring and reviewing the performance and effectiveness of the BCMS;
- continual improvement based on qualitative and quantitative measures.

A BCMS, like any other management system, includes the following components:

a) a policy;
b) competent people with defined responsibilities;
c) management processes relating to:
    1) policy;
    2) planning;
    3) implementation and operation;
    4) performance assessment;
    5) management review;
    6) continual improvement;

d) documented information supporting operational control and enabling performance evaluation."

The standard also defines the benefits of a BCMS as "The purpose of a BCMS is to prepare for, provide and maintain controls and capabilities for managing an organization's overall ability to continue to operate during disruptions. In achieving this, the organization is:

a) from a business perspective:

1) supporting its strategic objectives;
2) creating a competitive advantage;
3) protecting and enhancing its reputation and credibility;
4) contributing to organizational resilience;

b) from a financial perspective:
1) reducing legal and financial exposure;
2) reducing direct and indirect costs of disruptions;

c) from the perspective of interested parties:
1) protecting life, property and the environment;
2) considering the expectations of interested parties;
3) providing confidence in the organization's ability to succeed;

d) from an internal processes' perspective:
1) improving its capability to remain effective during disruptions;
2) demonstrating proactive control of risks effectively and efficiently;
3) addressing operational vulnerabilities."

The standard, as such, does not talk a lot about TPRM directly, but has clear requirements (not expectations, this is a certifiable standard and has the 'requirements/ specifications') with respect to identification of internal and external dependencies and risk management.

Clause 8.1 mentions "The organization shall ensure that outsourced processes and the supply chain are controlled."

ISO 27001

ISO 27001 is an international standard for Information Security Management Systems (ISMS). It provides a systematic approach to managing sensitive company information so that it remains secure. This includes people, processes, and IT systems by applying a risk management process.

1. **Information Security Policy and Objectives**:
   - o Organisations should establish an information security policy and objectives that align with business requirements and security needs. TPRM must be integrated into these policies and objectives to ensure that third parties comply with the organization's information security requirements.
2. **Risk Assessment and Treatment**:
   - o Organisations should conduct regular risk assessments to identify and evaluate information security risks. This involves assessing the risks associated with third-party relationships and determining the appropriate risk treatment measures to mitigate those risks.
3. **Supplier Relationships**:
   - o Organisations should manage and monitor third-party access to organizational assets and information. Organizations must ensure that third parties meet the security requirements stipulated in their agreements.
4. **Security Controls Implementation**:
   - o Organizations must ensure that security controls are extended to third parties, especially those handling sensitive information or critical systems.
5. **Compliance and Legal Requirements**:
   - o Organisations should identify and comply with applicable legal, regulatory, and contractual requirements. Third parties should also adhere to these requirements, reducing compliance and legal risks.
6. **Monitoring, Review, and Auditing**:
   - o Organisations should regularly monitor, review, and audit the ISMS (Information Security Management System). This should be extended to third parties also to ensure ongoing protection and identify any potential issues.
7. **Incident Management**:
   - o Organisations should establish and maintain procedures for managing information security incidents. This is equally applicable to third parties whose incident management processes should be aligned with the organization's own incident response procedures.
8. **Documentation and Evidence**:

- o Third parties are required to provide evidence of compliance through assessments, agreements, performance data, and compliance records.

9. **Access Control**:
   - o Third parties should have appropriate access controls to protect sensitive information from unauthorized access or disclosure.

10. **Awareness and Training**:
    - o Organisations should extend their training and awareness programs to their third parties so that they understand and comply with the organization's information security policies and procedures.

ISO 9001

ISO 9001 is an international standard that specifies requirements for a quality management system (QMS). Organizations use the standard to demonstrate their ability to consistently provide products and services that meet customer and regulatory requirements. This standard is equally applicable to all industries.

1. **Supplier Quality Management**:
   - o Organizations should control their external providers to ensure that the products and services they procure meet specified requirements.
2. **Risk-Based Thinking**:
   - o Organisations should follow risk-based thinking. Organizations must identify and address risks and opportunities that can affect the conformity of products and services. This automatically gets extended to the third parties also.
3. **Evaluation and Selection of Suppliers**:
   - o Organizations must establish criteria for the evaluation, selection, monitoring, and re-evaluation of external providers.
4. **Monitoring and Measurement**:
   - o Organizations should monitor and measure the performance of their QMS, including the performance of external providers.
5. **Documented Information**:
   - o Organisations must maintain documented information to support the operation of processes and to provide evidence of conformity. In TPRM, documenting third-party assessments, contracts, performance data, and compliance information is crucial for transparency and accountability.
6. **Continual Improvement**:
   - o Organizations must seek opportunities to enhance their processes, including those involving third parties.
7. **Communication and Relationship Management**:
   - o Effective communication and relationship management with external providers are essential components of ISO 9001.

ISO 28000

ISO 28000 is an international standard that specifies requirements for a security management system, including aspects relevant to the supply chain.

1. **Supply Chain Security**:
   - o Organisations should establish, implement, maintain, and improve a security management system for the supply chain.
2. **Risk Assessment and Management**:
   - o Organizations should identify potential security threats, assess vulnerabilities, and implement appropriate controls to manage risks, including for their third-party relationships.
3. **Supplier and Contractor Security**:
   - o Organizations should ensure that their suppliers and contractors adhere to security requirements.
4. **Security Policies and Procedures**:
   - o Organizations must develop and implement security policies and procedures as part of ISO 28000 compliance. These policies and procedures should extend to third parties, ensuring that they follow the same security protocols.
5. **Incident Management**:
   - o Organisations should detect, report, and respond to security incidents. This gets extended to third parties, and they should have robust incident management processes in place.
6. **Compliance and Legal Requirements**:

- o Organizations should comply with applicable legal and regulatory requirements related to supply chain security.

Chapter 5. Developing a TPRM Program

Developing a TPRM program involves:

- **Defining Objectives:** Setting clear goals and objectives for the program.

Defining Objectives

Defining clear goals and objectives is the foundational step in developing a robust Third Party Risk Management (TPRM) program. This step ensures that the program is aligned with the organization's strategic priorities and provides a clear direction for all subsequent activities.

Setting Clear Goals and Objectives

Identifying Key Objectives

The first step in defining objectives is to identify the key goals of the TPRM program. This involves understanding the primary reasons for establishing the program and what it aims to achieve. Common objectives include protecting sensitive data, ensuring compliance with regulations, mitigating operational risks, and enhancing overall business resilience.

To ensure these objectives are well-defined and actionable, they should be specific, measurable, achievable, relevant, and time-bound (SMART). Below, I provide sample SMART objectives for the TPRM Program:

Reduce High-Risk Vendors: Reduce the number of high-risk vendors by 20% within the first year by implementing enhanced due diligence and risk mitigation strategies.

Enhance Vendor Compliance: Achieve 95% compliance of critical vendors with the organization's security policies and regulatory requirements within 18 months.

Improve Risk Assessment Coverage: Conduct comprehensive risk assessments for 100% of new high-risk vendors within 30 days of engagement and reassess all existing high-risk vendors annually.

Decrease Incident Response Time: Reduce the average incident response time for third party-related security breaches by 50% within 12 months through improved monitoring and response protocols.

Increase Employee Training Participation: Ensure that 90% of employees involved in third-party management complete TPRM training programs within the next six months.

Strengthen Cybersecurity Posture: Implement cybersecurity assessments for all third-party vendors with access to sensitive data, achieving a 30% increase in the number of vendors with a robust cybersecurity posture within one year.

Enhance Risk Mitigation Plans: Develop and implement risk mitigation plans for all identified high-risk vendors, achieving a 100% completion rate within 12 months.

Boost Vendor Performance Monitoring: Establish a performance monitoring framework for critical vendors, aiming for a 20% improvement in vendor performance metrics (e.g., service delivery, compliance) within the next year.

Increase Audit Frequency: Conduct audits of 50% of high-risk vendors biannually to ensure adherence to contractual obligations and compliance requirements within 24 months.

Improve Third-Party Data Protection: Achieve a 40% reduction in third-party data breaches within two years by implementing stricter data protection policies and regular security audits.

Supplier Onboarding Compliance: Ensure 100% of new suppliers complete the TPRM onboarding process, including risk assessments and compliance checks, within 45 days of engagement within the next year.

Supplier Performance Improvement: Increase the overall performance rating of suppliers by 25% within 18 months through enhanced performance monitoring, feedback mechanisms, and targeted improvement plans.

Sustainability Initiatives: Achieve a 30% increase in the number of suppliers meeting the organization's sustainability and environmental standards within two years by implementing a supplier sustainability assessment program.

Partner Risk Assessment: Conduct comprehensive risk assessments for 100% of new strategic partners within 60 days of engagement and reassess all existing partners annually to ensure alignment with organizational risk tolerance within the next year.

Enhance Data Security Practices: Ensure that 95% of strategic partners with access to sensitive data implement and maintain robust data security practices within 12 months by providing guidelines and conducting regular security audits.

Increase Partner Collaboration: Increase collaborative initiatives with strategic partners by 40% within the next 18 months to enhance mutual risk mitigation efforts and align business continuity plans.

Aligning Objectives with Business Strategy

For a TPRM program to be effective, its objectives must align with the overall business strategy. This alignment ensures that the program supports the broader goals of the organization and secures buy-in from senior leadership.

Engaging with key stakeholders across the organization, including senior executives, department heads, and functional leaders, is essential in this process. Through these discussions, one can ensure that the TPRM objectives resonate with the strategic priorities of different business units and gain their support and commitment.

Determining Risk Appetite and Tolerance

A critical aspect of defining objectives is determining the organization's risk appetite and tolerance levels. Risk appetite refers to the amount and type of risk an organization is willing to accept to achieve its objectives, while risk tolerance defines the acceptable level of variation in achieving these objectives.

By clearly defining these parameters, the TPRM program can prioritize risks appropriately and implement controls that are proportionate to the organization's willingness to accept risk. This clarity helps in decision-making and ensures that risk management efforts are aligned with the organization's strategic goals.

- **Stakeholder Engagement:** Involving key stakeholders from various departments.

Stakeholder Engagement

Effective stakeholder engagement is crucial to the success of any Third Party Risk Management (TPRM) program. Stakeholders, both internal and external, play a pivotal role in shaping the program, ensuring its smooth implementation, and driving continual improvement. In this chapter, we will explore strategies and best practices for engaging stakeholders throughout the TPRM lifecycle.

Identifying and Prioritizing Stakeholders

The first step in stakeholder engagement is identifying who your stakeholders are and prioritizing them based on their influence, interest, and impact on the TPRM program.

Identifying Stakeholders

Creating a comprehensive list of stakeholders involves recognizing all potential individuals and groups that might affect or be affected by the TPRM program. This list typically includes internal departments such as procurement, legal, IT, finance, and business unit leaders, as well as external partners like key vendors, suppliers, and partners. My 'Interested Parties Management Cycle' will be helpful:

Prioritizing Stakeholders

Once one has identified their stakeholders, the next step is to prioritize them. A useful tool for this process is the influence and interest matrix. This matrix helps categorize stakeholders based on their level of influence over the program and their interest in its outcomes. By focusing first on those with high influence and high interest, you can ensure that you address the most critical stakeholders' needs and concerns early in the process.

Roles in TPRM

Different roles in Third Party Risk Management (TPRM) encompass various levels of responsibility and focus, ranging from strategic oversight to operational execution. Here are some key roles typically found in TPRM:

Strategic Roles

1. **Chief Risk Officer (CRO)**
   - Oversees the organization's risk management strategy, including third-party risks.
   - Ensures alignment with overall business objectives and regulatory requirements.
2. **Chief Compliance Officer (CCO)**
   - Ensures that the organization complies with all relevant laws and regulations related to third-party relationships.
   - Develops and implements compliance policies and procedures.
3. **Chief Vendor Data Manager**
   - Manages vendor data and ensures compliance with confidentiality and security standards.
   - Implements strategies to mitigate data-related risks associated with third parties.

Managerial Roles

4. **Vendor Risk Manager**
   o Identifies, assesses, and mitigates risks associated with third-party vendors.
   o Develops and maintains vendor risk management policies and procedures.
5. **Vendor Relationship Manager**
   o Manages relationships with third-party vendors to ensure performance and compliance with agreements.
   o Acts as a liaison between the organization and vendors, addressing issues and concerns.
6. **Risk Management Analyst**
   o Conducts risk assessments and analyses of third-party vendors.
   o Monitors vendor performance and compliance with risk management policies.

Operational Roles

7. **Third-Party Risk Assessor**
   o Evaluates the risk profiles of potential and existing vendors.
   o Performs due diligence and ongoing monitoring to ensure vendors meet risk management criteria.
8. **Compliance Analyst**
   o Assists in the development and implementation of compliance programs for third-party risk.
   o Monitors vendor activities to ensure adherence to regulatory and contractual obligations.
9. **IT Security Specialist**
   o Focuses on the cybersecurity aspects of third-party risk management.
   o Ensures vendors comply with the organization's IT security policies and standards.
10. **Procurement Specialist**
   o Manages the procurement process, ensuring vendors are selected based on risk assessments.
   o Works with risk management teams to incorporate risk mitigation strategies in vendor contracts.

Support Roles

11. **Administrative Staff**
   o Handles administrative tasks related to vendor management, such as documentation and record-keeping.
   o Supports the operational aspects of TPRM by maintaining organized and accessible records.
12. **Training and Development Coordinator**
   o Develops and delivers training programs for employees on third-party risk management policies and procedures.
   o Ensures staff are aware of and understand TPRM protocols.

Advisory Roles

13. **External Auditors**
   o Conduct independent assessments of the organization's third-party risk management practices.
   o Provide recommendations for improving TPRM processes and controls.
14. **Legal Advisors**
   o Offer legal guidance on third-party contracts, compliance issues, and risk mitigation strategies.
   o Ensure that vendor agreements are legally sound and protect the organization's interests.

These roles collaborate to create a comprehensive TPRM framework that addresses the complexities and risks associated with third-party relationships.

Influence and Interest Matrix

The matrix consists of four quadrants:

1. **High Influence, High Interest** (Manage Closely)
2. **High Influence, Low Interest** (Keep Satisfied)
3. **Low Influence, High Interest** (Keep Informed)

4. **Low Influence, Low Interest** (Monitor)

Here is a visual representation of the matrix:

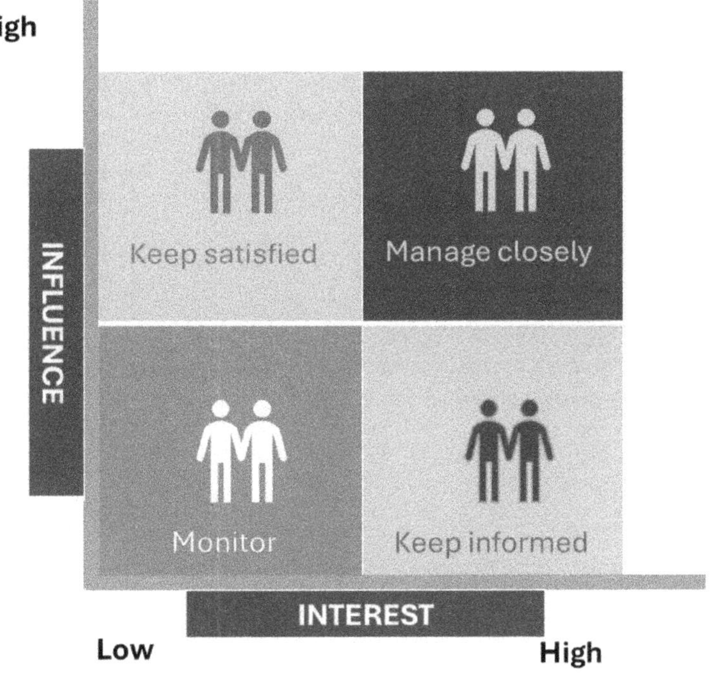

Example Stakeholder Categorization

High Interest - High Influence

Roles:

- **Chief Risk Officer (CRO):** Has a significant stake in the risk management framework and can influence organizational strategies and policies.
- **Chief Vendor Data Manager:** Directly involved in managing vendor relationships and ensuring compliance with NDAs and other risk management practices.
- **Board of Directors:** Interested in the overall risk profile and governance of third-party relationships, with the authority to make high-level decisions.

High Interest - Low Influence

Roles:

- **Risk Management Analysts:** Deeply involved in the day-to-day operations of TPRM, analyzing data, and assessing risks, but with limited decision-making power.
- **Vendor Relationship Managers:** Directly engaged with vendors, ensuring compliance and managing performance, but not in a position to influence broader organizational strategies.

Low Interest - High Influence

Roles:

- **Chief Financial Officer (CFO):** May not be directly interested in the specifics of TPRM but has the power to allocate resources and influence major decisions affecting the program.
- **Chief Operating Officer (COO):** Focused on operational efficiency and may influence TPRM processes and policies, though not necessarily deeply invested in the details.

Low Interest - Low Influence

Roles:

- **IT Support Staff:** Provide necessary support for TPRM tools and systems but have little interest in or influence over the strategic aspects of TPRM.
- **Junior Administrative Staff:** Handle administrative tasks related to vendor management with minimal interest in or impact on the overall risk management framework.

These examples help illustrate how different roles fit within the Influence-Interest Matrix in the context of TPRM, highlighting the varying degrees of interest and influence each role possesses.[i]

Understanding Stakeholder Needs and Expectations

To engage stakeholders effectively, it is essential to understand their needs, expectations, and concerns. This involves conducting thorough stakeholder analysis and aligning the TPRM program's objectives with stakeholder interests.

Conducting Stakeholder Analysis

Stakeholder analysis involves gathering detailed information about each stakeholder group. Techniques such as surveys and interviews can be particularly useful for this purpose. By asking stakeholders about their expectations, concerns, and what they hope to achieve from the TPRM program, you can gain valuable insights that will inform your engagement strategy.

Aligning Objectives

Aligning the objectives of the TPRM program with the interests of your stakeholders helps to ensure mutual benefits. For instance, a procurement team might be interested in reducing supplier risks, while the IT department might focus on cybersecurity. By addressing these specific interests within the TPRM framework, you can secure stronger support and cooperation from these groups. Proactively addressing any concerns raised by stakeholders will also help build trust and foster a collaborative environment.

Developing a Communication Plan

A well-thought-out communication plan is a cornerstone of effective stakeholder engagement. This plan should outline the communication objectives, key messages, and the channels through which you will keep stakeholders informed and involved. My Communication Cycle is in alignment with the requirements of clause 7 of ISO 22301:2019:

Creating a Communication Strategy

Start by defining clear communication objectives. These might include raising awareness about the TPRM program, securing buy-in from key stakeholders, or providing regular updates on progress and challenges. Next, develop key messages tailored to the interests and concerns of each stakeholder group. For example, for the finance team, emphasize the program's role in reducing financial risks and ensuring compliance with regulatory requirements.

Choosing Appropriate Channels

Selecting the right communication channels is crucial for effective engagement. Consider the preferences and habits of each stakeholder group. Email updates, newsletters, and intranet portals can be useful for broad communications, while regular meetings or briefings might be more effective for high-priority stakeholders. Determine the appropriate frequency of communication to keep stakeholders informed without overwhelming them.

For ease of my readers, I am giving below two sample communications that may be customized and used:

Sample Internal Communication Email

Subject: Launch of Our New Third Party Risk Management (TPRM) Program

Dear Team,

I am pleased to announce the launch of our new Third Party Risk Management (TPRM) program, effective immediately. This initiative is a critical component of our strategy to enhance organizational resilience and safeguard our operations from potential risks associated with third-party relationships.

Objectives of the TPRM Program:

1. **Risk Identification and Mitigation:** Systematically identify, assess, and mitigate risks associated with third-party vendors.
2. **Compliance and Security:** Ensure compliance with regulatory requirements and enhance the security of our data and operations.
3. **Vendor Performance Management:** Foster robust partnerships with our vendors to ensure consistent performance and adherence to agreed standards.

Your Role:

- **Engagement:** Participate in training sessions and familiarize yourself with the TPRM policies and procedures.
- **Collaboration:** Work closely with the Risk Management and Vendor Relationship teams to ensure smooth implementation and operation of the TPRM program.

- **Reporting:** Immediately report any concerns or potential risks related to third parties to your supervisor or the Risk Management team.

We will be conducting a series of training sessions and workshops in the coming weeks to provide detailed insights into the TPRM framework and your role within it. Your active participation and cooperation are crucial for the success of this program.

For any questions or further information, please do not hesitate to contact the Risk Management team.

Thank you for your attention and commitment to enhancing our organizational resilience.

Best regards,
[Your Name]
Chief Risk Officer
[Company Name]

Sample Communication Email for Third Parties

Subject: Introduction of Our Third Party Risk Management (TPRM) Program

Dear [Vendor/ Supplier/ Partner Name],

We are excited to inform you about the launch of our new Third Party Risk Management (TPRM) program, which is now in effect. This program is designed to strengthen our collaborative efforts and ensure that our partnerships are both secure and mutually beneficial.

Key Objectives of the TPRM Program:

1. **Risk Management:** Identify and manage risks associated with our third-party relationships to ensure continuity and security in our operations.
2. **Compliance and Security:** Ensure compliance with relevant regulations and enhance the protection of sensitive information.
3. **Performance Monitoring:** Monitor and support vendor performance to maintain high standards and achieve common goals.

What This Means for You:

- **Enhanced Collaboration:** We will be working closely with you to ensure compliance with our risk management policies and procedures.
- **Regular Assessments:** Expect periodic assessments and reviews to identify potential risks and areas for improvement.
- **Support and Guidance:** Our Vendor Relationship and Risk Management teams will provide ongoing support and guidance to help you meet the TPRM requirements.

We believe that this program will significantly benefit both parties by fostering a transparent and secure working environment. Your cooperation and commitment are essential to the success of this initiative.

If you have any questions or need further information, please feel free to reach out to our Vendor Relationship Manager at [Contact Information].

Thank you for your partnership and support.

Best regards,
[Your Name]
Chief Risk Officer
[Company Name]

These emails should set a clear and professional tone, outlining the importance and objectives of the TPRM program and detailing the expectations for both internal team members and third-party vendors.

Engaging Stakeholders Early and Often

Early and ongoing engagement of stakeholders is critical to the success of the TPRM program. By involving stakeholders from the beginning and maintaining regular interaction, you can build a sense of ownership and ensure continuous support.

Early Involvement

Involve key stakeholders in the initial stages of the TPRM program development. This can be achieved through initial meetings, workshops, and seminars designed to educate stakeholders about the importance and benefits of the program. Early involvement helps to gather valuable input and build a sense of ownership among stakeholders.

Ongoing Engagement

Maintain regular engagement with stakeholders throughout the TPRM lifecycle. Provide consistent updates on the progress of the program, any changes or developments, and solicit feedback during feedback sessions. This ongoing dialogue helps to keep stakeholders informed, address any emerging concerns, and reinforce their commitment to the program.

Defining Clear Roles and Responsibilities

Clear definition of roles and responsibilities is essential for effective stakeholder engagement. This clarity helps to ensure that everyone understands their role within the TPRM program and contributes effectively.

Role Clarity

Clearly define the roles and responsibilities of each stakeholder within the TPRM program. For example, the procurement team might be responsible for integrating third-party risk considerations into the procurement process, while the IT department handles cybersecurity assessments and monitoring. Establish accountability mechanisms to ensure that stakeholders understand and fulfill their roles.

Role-Based Training

Provide tailored training sessions for different stakeholder groups based on their roles and responsibilities. This training helps to equip stakeholders with the knowledge and skills they need to perform their roles effectively. Encourage continuous learning and development to keep stakeholders updated on best practices and emerging risks.

Building Strong Relationships

Building strong relationships with stakeholders is fundamental to the success of the TPRM program. Trust and collaboration are key components of these relationships.

Trust Building

Transparency, honesty, and integrity are the cornerstones of trust building. Be transparent about the goals, processes, and challenges of the TPRM program. Maintain honesty and integrity in all interactions to build and sustain trust with stakeholders.

Collaboration

Foster a collaborative approach by involving stakeholders in decision-making and problem-solving processes. Emphasize shared goals and the collective benefits of a successful TPRM program. This collaborative mindset helps to create a sense of unity and common purpose among stakeholders.

Leveraging Technology and Tools

Leveraging technology and tools can enhance stakeholder engagement by streamlining communication and collaboration processes.

Using Engagement Tools

Stakeholder management software can help track interactions, feedback, and engagement levels. Communication platforms such as Slack, Microsoft Teams, or project management tools can facilitate collaboration and ensure that stakeholders remain connected and informed.

Automating Processes

Automation can improve consistency and efficiency in stakeholder engagement. Automated processes, such as sending updates or reminders, help ensure that stakeholders receive timely and relevant information.

Monitoring and Evaluating Engagement

Regular monitoring and evaluation of stakeholder engagement efforts are essential to ensure their effectiveness and to identify areas for improvement.

Measuring Engagement

Develop metrics to measure stakeholder engagement, such as participation rates, feedback quality, and satisfaction levels. Regularly review these metrics to evaluate the effectiveness of your engagement strategy.

Continual Improvement

Use insights from engagement metrics and feedback to adjust and improve your stakeholder engagement strategies. Continuously learn from successful engagements and adapt your approach to address any challenges or gaps.

By following these strategies and good practices, you can ensure effective stakeholder engagement, which is vital for the success and sustainability of your TPRM program. Engaged stakeholders are more likely to support the program, contribute valuable insights, and collaborate to mitigate third-party risks effectively.

- **Policy Development:** Creating policies and procedures for managing third-party risks.

Policy Development

Creating comprehensive policies and procedures is a crucial step in managing third-party risks. These policies provide a structured approach to risk management and ensure consistency in how third-party risks are identified, assessed, and mitigated across the organization.

Developing Policies and Procedures

Risk Assessment Policies

Developing policies for risk assessment involves outlining the criteria and processes for evaluating third-party risks. This includes defining the types of risks to be assessed (e.g., financial, operational, cybersecurity), the methods for assessing these risks, and the frequency of assessments.

Policies should also specify the criteria for categorizing third parties based on their risk levels. For example, vendors can be classified as low, medium, or high risk based on factors such as the criticality of the services they provide, their access to sensitive data, and their compliance with regulatory requirements.

Due Diligence Procedures

Due diligence procedures outline the steps for conducting thorough background checks and evaluations of third parties. These procedures should include:

- **Background Checks:** Verifying the third party's financial stability, legal history, and business reputation.
- **Security Assessments:** Assessing the third party's information security controls and practices to ensure they meet the organization's standards.
- **Compliance Reviews:** Ensuring the third party complies with relevant regulations and industry standards.

Due diligence should be conducted before engaging a new third party and periodically throughout the duration of the relationship to identify any changes in the risk profile.

Policy Approval and Implementation

Once the policies and procedures are developed, they need to be reviewed and approved by relevant stakeholders and governance bodies. This step ensures that the policies are comprehensive, feasible, and aligned with the organization's strategic objectives.

After approval, the next step is implementation. This involves communicating the policies to all relevant employees and third parties, providing training to ensure understanding and compliance, and integrating the policies into existing business processes and systems.

Training and Awareness

Training and awareness programs are essential to ensure that all employees and third parties understand and adhere to the TPRM policies and procedures. Regular training sessions should be conducted to educate employees about their roles and responsibilities in managing third-party risks and to keep them updated on any changes in policies or procedures.

- **Program Governance:** Establishing a governance structure to oversee the program.

Program Governance

Establishing a robust governance structure is critical to oversee the TPRM program effectively. Governance provides the framework for decision-making, accountability, and continuous improvement, ensuring that the program remains aligned with organizational objectives and adapts to changing risk landscapes.

Establishing Governance Structure

Governance Committee

A governance committee or steering group should be established to provide oversight and strategic direction for the TPRM program. This committee should include senior executives and representatives from key departments such as procurement, legal, IT, finance, and compliance.

The governance committee's responsibilities include:

- **Setting Strategic Direction:** Defining the strategic objectives and priorities of the TPRM program.
- **Resource Allocation:** Ensuring that adequate resources (budget, personnel, technology) are allocated to the program.
- **Policy Approval:** Reviewing and approving TPRM policies and procedures.

Defining Roles and Responsibilities

Clear roles and responsibilities should be defined for all members of the governance structure. This includes:

- **Executive Sponsor:** Typically, a C-level executive who champions the TPRM program and ensures it receives necessary support and resources.
- **Program Manager:** An individual responsible for the day-to-day management of the TPRM program, including coordination, communication, and implementation.
- **Departmental Representatives:** Individuals from key departments who provide expertise and ensure that departmental interests are represented in the program.

Monitoring and Reporting

Performance Metrics

Developing key performance indicators (KPIs) is essential for monitoring the effectiveness of the TPRM program. These metrics should measure various aspects of the program, such as the number of third-party assessments conducted, the percentage of high-risk vendors identified, and the effectiveness of risk mitigation measures.

Regular monitoring of these KPIs helps to identify areas where the program is performing well and areas that may need improvement. It also provides valuable data for reporting to senior management and the governance committee.

Regular Reporting

Implementing regular reporting mechanisms is crucial for keeping the governance committee and stakeholders informed about the program's performance and risks. Regular reports should include:

- **Risk Assessment Results:** Summaries of the latest risk assessments and any changes in third-party risk profiles.
- **Compliance Status:** Updates on third-party compliance with relevant policies, procedures, and regulations.
- **Program Performance:** Analysis of KPIs and progress towards achieving program objectives.

These reports help ensure transparency, facilitate informed decision-making, and support continuous improvement of the TPRM program.

Continual Improvement

Continual improvement is a vital aspect of a successful TPRM program. It involves regularly reviewing and refining the program to address new risks, incorporate best practices, and respond to changes in the business environment.

Feedback Loop

Establishing a feedback loop is essential for capturing lessons learned and identifying areas for improvement. Feedback can be gathered through:

- **Stakeholder Input:** Regularly soliciting input from stakeholders to understand their experiences and suggestions for improvement.
- **Program Reviews:** Conducting periodic reviews of the TPRM program to assess its effectiveness and identify any gaps or weaknesses.

Continual Learning

Encouraging continual learning and development helps to ensure that the TPRM program remains up to date with emerging risks and best practices. This can be achieved through:

- **Training Programs:** Regular training sessions for employees and third parties to keep them informed about new risks, regulatory changes, and best practices.

- **Industry Engagement:** Participating in industry forums, conferences, and working groups to stay abreast of the latest developments in third-party risk management.

By following these strategies and best practices for defining objectives, developing policies, and establishing governance structures, you can build a robust and effective TPRM program that helps your organization manage third-party risks comprehensively and proactively.

Chapter 6: Integrating TPRM with Enterprise Risk Management (ERM)

Introduction

Integrating Third Party Risk Management (TPRM) with Enterprise Risk Management (ERM) ensures a comprehensive and unified approach to risk management. This integration helps organizations align their TPRM objectives with overall risk management goals, leverage existing ERM tools and frameworks, and maintain consistency in risk management practices across the organization. This chapter provides a comprehensive guide to integrating TPRM with ERM, including practical steps, examples, and best practices.

The Importance of Integrating TPRM with ERM

Integrating TPRM with ERM offers several key benefits:

- **Holistic Risk View**: Provides a unified view of risks across the enterprise, including third-party risks.
- **Enhanced Decision-Making**: Facilitates better-informed decision-making by incorporating third-party risks into the overall risk landscape.
- **Resource Optimization**: Improves resource allocation by aligning TPRM efforts with broader risk management priorities.
- **Regulatory Compliance**: Helps ensure compliance with regulatory requirements by providing a comprehensive risk management framework.

Aligning Objectives

1. Establishing a Common Risk Framework

To integrate TPRM with ERM, organizations should establish a common risk framework that encompasses all types of risks, including third-party risks. This involves:

- Defining risk categories and criteria that apply to both TPRM and ERM.
- Establishing a unified risk appetite and tolerance levels that consider third-party risks.
- Developing a common risk assessment methodology to evaluate all risks consistently.

2. Setting Aligned Risk Management Goals

Aligning TPRM objectives with ERM goals involves setting risk management goals that address both third-party and enterprise-wide risks. These goals should:

- Reflect the organization's overall risk management strategy.
- Address specific third-party risk factors, such as vendor reliability, compliance, and cybersecurity.
- Ensure that third-party risks are considered in strategic planning and decision-making processes.

Leveraging Tools

1. Utilizing ERM Tools for TPRM

Organizations can leverage existing ERM tools and frameworks to enhance their TPRM processes. This includes:

- **Risk Assessment Tools**: Using ERM risk assessment tools to evaluate third-party risks in conjunction with other enterprise risks.
- **Risk Registers**: Incorporating third-party risks into the organization's risk register to ensure they are tracked and managed alongside other risks.

- **Risk Dashboards**: Integrating third-party risk metrics into ERM dashboards to provide a comprehensive view of the organization's risk profile.

2. Adopting Advanced Technologies

Advanced technologies, such as AI and machine learning, can be utilized to enhance both TPRM and ERM. These technologies can (I have devoted a separate chapter in the book on this topic):

- Analyze large volumes of data to identify emerging risks.
- Provide predictive analytics to forecast potential risk events.
- Automate routine risk management tasks, such as data collection and analysis.

Ensuring Consistency

1. Standardizing Risk Management Practices

Ensuring consistency in risk management practices involves standardizing processes and methodologies across the organization. This includes:

- Developing standardized risk assessment templates that can be used for both third-party and enterprise-wide risks.
- Implementing consistent risk scoring and rating systems to evaluate risks uniformly.
- Establishing uniform risk reporting procedures to ensure that third-party risks are reported in the same manner as other risks.

2. Coordinating Risk Management Activities

Coordinating risk management activities across different departments and functions is essential for maintaining consistency. This involves:

- Creating cross-functional risk management teams that include representatives from TPRM and ERM.
- Facilitating regular communication and collaboration between TPRM and ERM teams.
- Aligning risk management activities with organizational goals and priorities.

Practical Steps for Integration

The easiest way to say is to run this as a Change Program or a Transformation Program in the organization.

1. Conduct a Gap Analysis

Perform a gap analysis to identify discrepancies between TPRM and ERM practices. This involves:

- Assessing the current state of TPRM and ERM processes.
- Identifying areas where integration can be improved.
- Developing a roadmap to address identified gaps.

2. Develop an Integration Plan

Create a detailed plan to integrate TPRM with ERM. This plan should include:

- Specific objectives and goals for the integration.
- Key activities and milestones to achieve integration.
- Roles and responsibilities of team members involved in the integration process.

3. Implement the Integration

Implement the integration plan by:

- Aligning risk management policies and procedures.
- Integrating risk management tools and technologies.
- Providing training and support to ensure that team members understand and adhere to the integrated risk management processes.

4. Monitor and Review

Continuously monitor and review the integrated risk management framework to ensure its effectiveness. This involves:

- Conducting regular audits and assessments to evaluate the integration.
- Gathering feedback from stakeholders to identify areas for improvement.
- Updating the risk management framework as needed to address emerging risks and changing business conditions.

A word of caution again is that while there will be resource optimization through this integration, I do not at all mean to say that ERM can/ shall do TPRM also. Both programs have a lot to be done and a single person/ team many not be able to do a good job.

Good Practices for Integration

- **Engage Stakeholders**: Involve key stakeholders from across the organization in the integration process to ensure buy-in and support.
- **Leverage Technology**: Utilize advanced technologies, such as AI and machine learning, to enhance risk identification, assessment, and monitoring.
- **Continual Improvement**: Regularly review and update the integrated risk management framework to address new risks and evolving business needs.
- **Training and Awareness**: Provide ongoing training and awareness programs to ensure that all team members understand and adhere to the integrated risk management processes. Theoretically, your training and awareness program needs to be extended to your third parties also.

Conclusion

Integrating TPRM with ERM provides a comprehensive approach to risk management that enhances an organization's ability to identify, assess, mitigate, and monitor risks. By aligning objectives, leveraging tools, and ensuring consistency in risk management practices, organizations can create a unified risk management framework that addresses both third-party and enterprise-wide risks. This integration is essential for maintaining resilience, achieving regulatory compliance, and ensuring long-term success in today's dynamic business environment.

Chapter 7: Due Diligence and Onboarding

Conducting Due Diligence

Due diligence is a critical process that involves thoroughly evaluating third parties before engaging them in business activities. The goal is to identify and mitigate potential risks associated with the third party. This chapter provides a comprehensive guide to conducting due diligence, complete with detailed steps, checklists, tools, and templates to help streamline the process.

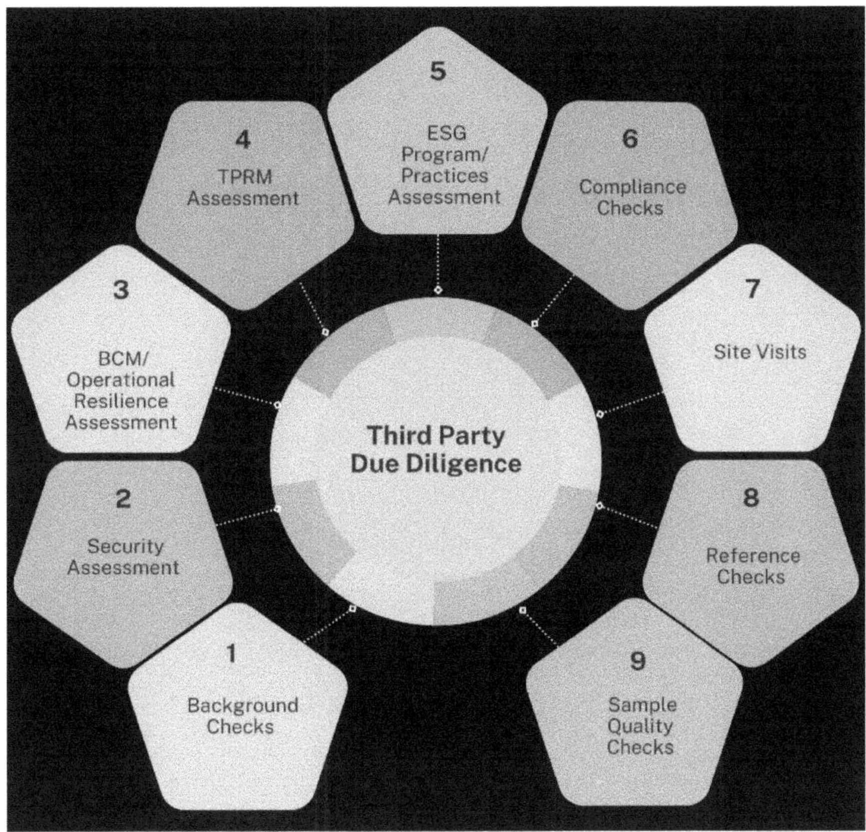

Background Checks

Background checks are essential to verify the third party's credentials, financial stability, and reputation. This involves several steps.

First, investigate the third party's history, including its establishment date, ownership structure, and key personnel. This ensures that you understand who you are dealing with and the background of the organization. Utilize public records databases and company registration websites to gather this information. Look for details such as the year of establishment, ownership details, and key management personnel.

Next, assess the financial stability of the third party by reviewing their financial statements, credit ratings, and any history of bankruptcy or financial difficulties. This step helps to ensure that the third party is financially sound and capable of meeting its obligations. Use financial analysis software and consult credit rating agencies to obtain a comprehensive view of their financial health. Key documents to review include financial statements from the last three years, credit ratings, and any records of financial difficulties.

Additionally, examine the third party's reputation in the market and any past or ongoing legal issues. This helps to identify any potential red flags that could affect your organization's reputation or operations. Media reports and legal databases are useful tools for this step. Key aspects to consider include the market reputation, any legal disputes, and the third party's regulatory compliance history.

Security Assessment

Assessing the third party's cybersecurity practices is crucial to ensure they have adequate measures in place to protect sensitive information and prevent breaches.

Begin by reviewing the third party's cybersecurity policies, procedures, and frameworks. This includes examining their cybersecurity policy document, incident response plan, and data protection measures. Utilizing cybersecurity assessment frameworks such as NIST or ISO 27001 can provide a structured approach to this review.

Evaluate the technical security measures implemented by the third party, such as firewalls, encryption, and access controls. This helps to ensure that they have robust defenses against cyber threats. Network security tools and penetration testing software can be used to assess these technical measures. Key areas to review include firewall configurations, encryption protocols, and access control mechanisms.

Ensure the third party runs adequate cybersecurity training and awareness programs for their employees. This is essential to minimize the risk of human error and to ensure that all employees are aware of cybersecurity best practices. Training platforms and awareness program materials can be used to evaluate the effectiveness of these programs.

Business Continuity Management (BCM) and Operational Resilience Assessment

Assess the third party's business continuity management and operational resilience programs to ensure they can maintain operations during disruptions.

Review their business continuity plans, disaster recovery plans, and resilience strategies. This includes evaluating their ability to continue critical business functions during adverse conditions. Key areas to review include the existence and robustness of business continuity plans, disaster recovery plans, and resilience strategies.

Understand their business continuity test procedures and achievements.

Verify the third party's track record in managing past disruptions and their capacity to recover from them. This involves examining incident response reports, historical performance data during disruptions, and any lessons learned from past incidents.

Third Party Risk Management (TPRM) Assessment

This is interesting! While conducting due diligence for your third party - evaluate their risk management practices, focusing on how they manage risks associated with their own third parties.

Assess their vendor management processes, risk assessment methodologies, and mitigation strategies. This ensures that they are not introducing additional risks through their third-party relationships. Review their risk assessment reports, vendor management policies, and risk mitigation plans to get a comprehensive understanding of their TPRM practices.

Environmental, Social, and Governance (ESG) Program/ Practices Assessment

Assess the third party's adherence to ESG program/ practices to ensure they align with your organization's values and regulatory requirements.

Review their environmental policies, social responsibility initiatives, and governance structures. This helps to ensure that they are operating in a sustainable and ethical manner. Key areas to review include their environmental impact assessments, CSR reports, and governance frameworks.

Evaluate their performance in key ESG areas such as carbon footprint, labor practices, diversity and inclusion, and anti-corruption measures. This involves examining their ESG performance reports, sustainability certifications, and any third-party audits or assessments.

Compliance Checks

Ensuring the third party complies with relevant regulations and standards is vital to mitigate regulatory risks and avoid potential penalties.

Verify that the third party complies with industry-specific regulations and standards. This includes reviewing compliance certificates and audit reports. Compliance management software and regulatory databases can be useful tools in this step. Key aspects to consider include industry-specific regulations, compliance certificates, and audit reports.

Assess the third party's adherence to ethical standards and corporate social responsibility (CSR) practices. This helps to ensure that the third party operates ethically and aligns with your organization's values. CSR reporting tools and ethics audit frameworks can be used to evaluate these aspects. Key areas to review include the code of ethics, CSR initiatives, and anti-corruption policies.

Evaluate the third party's data protection and privacy practices to ensure they comply with data protection laws such as GDPR, CCPA, etc. This is essential to protect sensitive information and avoid potential legal issues. Data protection impact assessment tools and privacy management software can be used to assess these practices. Key areas to review include data protection policies, privacy impact assessments, and the third party's history of data breaches.

In all assessments the approach should be to see the third party's Intent, Implementation, and Effectiveness.

The above can be performed based on inputs/ documents received from the third party and by reviewing them offsite (from your own office). The next level is to do some physical checks.

Site Visits

Conducting site visits allows you to observe the third party's operations firsthand and verify the information provided during the due diligence process.

Plan and conduct site visits to the third party's operational facilities. This helps to assess their operational capabilities, infrastructure, and overall environment. During the site visits, observe their processes, equipment, and working conditions. Key aspects to consider include the cleanliness and safety of the facilities, the condition of equipment, and the overall operational environment.

Engage with key personnel during the site visits to gather additional insights. This involves interviewing managers and employees to understand their practices and procedures better. Key areas to focus on include their operational processes, quality control measures, and any potential areas of concern observed during the visit.

These may appear to be more relevant to product outsourcing but are equally applicable to services outsourcing also.

Reference Checks

Reference checks are essential to validate the third party's performance and reliability through feedback from their existing or past clients.

Request references from the third party and conduct interviews with these references. This helps to gather information about their performance, reliability, and any potential issues. Key questions to ask include the reference's overall satisfaction with the third party, any issues encountered, and how these issues were resolved.

Use reference checks to corroborate the information provided by the third party and to gain a better understanding of their strengths and weaknesses. This step helps to ensure that you are making an informed decision based on real-world experiences of other clients.

Sample Quality Checks

Evaluating sample quality is crucial for ensuring that the third party meets your organization's quality standards.

Request and review samples of the third party's products or services. This helps to assess their quality, consistency, and adherence to specifications. Key aspects to consider include the quality of materials used, the workmanship, and the overall finish. Focus that not only the end product or services, but also the inputs and processes are of good quality.

Conduct tests and assessments on the samples to verify their quality. This may involve laboratory testing, performance evaluations, or other relevant tests. Use the results of these tests to determine whether the third party meets your quality standards and can consistently deliver products or services that meet your requirements.

An ultimate step may be to take a sample from the third party and take it through the full lifecycle at your end to see your finished goods and services.

Guidelines to Conducting Due Diligence

This section provides a step-by-step guide to conducting due diligence.

Preparation is the first step. Define the scope and objectives of the due diligence process. Identify the key areas of focus and assemble the due diligence team. This ensures that the process is well-organized and that all relevant aspects are covered. It is important to select your team appropriately, and your own assessment gadgets correctly.

Next, gather all necessary information and documentation from the third party. This includes requesting information from the third party, reviewing public records, and conducting interviews. This step is essential to obtain a comprehensive view of the third party's operations and risks.

Analyze the collected data to identify potential risks and issues. This includes financial analysis, risk assessment, and compliance review. This step helps to identify any potential red flags and to assess the overall risk associated with the third party.

Conduct site visits to observe the third party's operations firsthand and verify the information provided. Engage with key personnel and observe their processes and facilities.

Perform reference checks by requesting and interviewing references provided by the third party. This helps to validate their performance and reliability through feedback from existing or past clients.

Request and review samples of the third party's products or services to assess their quality. Conduct tests and assessments on the samples to verify their adherence to quality standards.

Compile the findings into a comprehensive due diligence report. This includes summarizing the findings, highlighting key risks, and providing recommendations. This report serves as a key document for decision-making and helps to ensure that all relevant information is considered.

Finally, use the due diligence report to make informed decisions about engaging the third party. This includes reviewing the report with stakeholders, making the engagement decision, and planning risk mitigation measures. This step ensures that the decision to engage the third party is based on a thorough understanding of the risks and that appropriate measures are in place to manage these risks.

Here I give my third tool on Third Party/ Vendor Management based on the above parameters.

1. **Background Checks**
   - Score: 1-5
     - 1: Poor background, multiple red flags
     - 2: Below average, some concerns
     - 3: Average, minor concerns
     - 4: Good, few concerns
     - 5: Excellent, no concerns
   - **Weightage**: 10%
2. **Security Assessment**
   - Score: 1-5
     - 1: Poor security practices, high risk
     - 2: Basic security practices, moderate risk
     - 3: Adequate security practices, some risk
     - 4: Good security practices, low risk
     - 5: Excellent security practices, no risk, certified to ISO 27001 and maintaining well
   - **Weightage**: 15%
3. **BCM/Operational Resilience Assessment**
   - Score: 1-5
     - 1: No BCM plan, high risk
     - 2: Basic BCM plan, moderate risk
     - 3: Adequate BCM plan, some risk
     - 4: Good BCM plan, low risk
     - 5: Comprehensive BCM plan, no risk, certified to ISO 22301 (or equivalent) and maintaining well
   - **Weightage**: 10%
4. **TPRM Assessment**
   - Score: 1-5
     - 1: Poor TPRM practices, high risk
     - 2: Basic TPRM practices, moderate risk
     - 3: Adequate TPRM practices, some risk
     - 4: Good TPRM practices, low risk
     - 5: Excellent TPRM practices, no risk
   - **Weightage**: 15%
5. **ESG Program/Practices Assessment**
   - Score: 1-5
     - 1: No ESG practices, high risk
     - 2: Basic ESG practices, moderate risk
     - 3: Adequate ESG practices, some risk
     - 4: Good ESG practices, low risk
     - 5: Comprehensive ESG practices, no risk, publishing reports on a regular basis
   - **Weightage**: 10%
6. **Compliance Checks**
   - Score: 1-5
     - 1: Non-compliance with major regulations
     - 2: Several compliance issues
     - 3: Compliant with most regulations, minor issues
     - 4: Compliant with all major regulations, minor recommendations
     - 5: Fully compliant, proactive in regulatory updates
   - **Weightage**: 10%
7. **Site Visits**
   - Score: 1-5
     - 1: Poor site conditions, high risk
     - 2: Below average site conditions, moderate risk
     - 3: Adequate site conditions, some risk
     - 4: Good site conditions, low risk
     - 5: Excellent site conditions, no risk, capability to provide required amounts
   - **Weightage**: 10%
8. **Reference Checks**
   - Score: 1-5

- - 1: No/ Poor references, negative feedback
    - 2: Few positive references, mixed feedback
    - 3: Some positive references, good feedback
    - 4: Many positive references, very good feedback
    - 5: Excellent references, outstanding feedback, awards, recognitions
  - **Weightage**: 10%
9. **Sample Quality Checks**
   - **Score**: 1-5
     - 1: Poor quality, many defects
     - 2: Below average quality, occasional defects
     - 3: Average quality, some defects
     - 4: Good quality, rare defects
     - 5: Excellent quality, no defects, great finished output
   - **Weightage**: 10%

Scoring Calculation

1. **Background Checks**: Score (1-5) × 5%
2. **Security Assessment**: Score (1-5) × 10%
3. **BCM/Operational Resilience Assessment**: Score (1-5) × 15%
4. **TPRM Assessment**: Score (1-5) × 15%
5. **ESG Program/Practices Assessment**: Score (1-5) × 10%
6. **Compliance Checks**: Score (1-5) × 10%
7. **Site Visits**: Score (1-5) × 10%
8. **Reference Checks**: Score (1-5) × 10%
9. **Sample Quality Checks**: Score (1-5) × 15%

Example of Total Scoring Sheet

Parameter	Score (1-5)	Weightage (%)	Weighted Score
Background Checks	4	5%	0.2
Security Assessment	5	10%	0.5
BCM/Operational Resilience Assessment	4	15%	0.6
TPRM Assessment	3	15%	0.45
ESG Program/Practices Assessment	5	10%	0.5
Compliance Checks	4	10%	0.4
Site Visits	4	10%	0.4
Reference Checks	3	10%	0.3
Sample Quality Checks	5	15%	0.75
Total		100%	**4.1**

The maximum possible score will be 5. The following decision tree may then be used

A third party scoring 3.75 and above = immediately approved

A third party scoring between 1.9 and 3.74 = ask to improve, reassess till they score 3.75 or above

A third party scoring below 1.9 = reject

Onboarding Third Parties

Once due diligence is complete and the decision to engage the third party has been made, the onboarding process begins. This process ensures that the third party is integrated into your organization's operations smoothly and that all necessary protocols and agreements are in place. This is similar to onboarding a new employee – a good recruit can be spoiled by poor onboarding experience! Replacing an employee is a costly affair – the same is true about a third party also. Both are relationships that need to be nurtured for optimum performance.

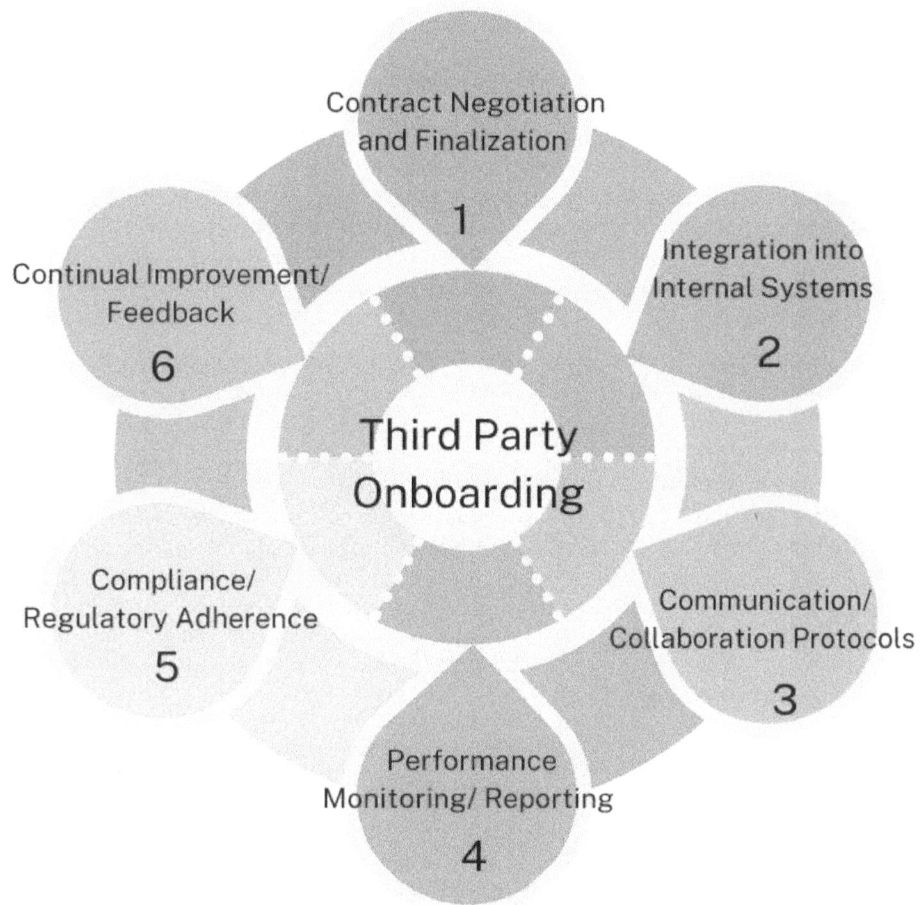

Contract Negotiation and Finalization

Negotiating and finalizing the contract with a third party is a critical step in the onboarding process. The contract should clearly outline the terms of the engagement, including the scope of work, deliverables, timelines, payment terms, confidentiality agreements, and any other relevant clauses.

- **Scope of Work:** Clearly define what work the third party is expected to perform. This includes detailed descriptions of tasks, responsibilities, expectations, specifications, tolerances etc.
- **Deliverables:** Specify the deliverables expected from the third party, including formats, deadlines, and quality standards.

- **Timelines:** Establish timelines for the completion of tasks and the delivery of products or services. Include milestones to track progress.
- **Payment Terms:** Outline payment terms, including the amount, payment schedule, and any conditions for payment.
- **Confidentiality Agreements:** Ensure that confidentiality agreements are in place to protect sensitive information.
- **Service Level Agreements:** Be as specific as you can be in writing various SLAs – do write for Business as Usual (BAU) and for BCM invocations.
- **Other Relevant Clauses:** Include clauses related to dispute resolution, termination conditions, and any other critical aspects.

Integration into Internal Systems

Integrating a third party into your internal systems is essential for seamless collaboration and communication.

- **Access to Systems:** Provide the third party with the necessary access to your systems and tools. This may include project management software, communication platforms, and any other relevant systems.
- **Training:** Conduct training sessions to ensure that the third party understands how to use your systems effectively. Provide documentation and support as needed.
- **Account Setup:** Set up accounts for the third party in your systems, including email, project management tools, and any other required platforms. Take care of duties, accesses etc. based on roles.

Communication and Collaboration Protocols

Establishing clear communication and collaboration protocols is crucial for maintaining effective coordination with the third party.

- **Communication Channels:** Define the primary communication channels for regular updates, queries, and issue resolution. This may include email, instant messaging, video conferencing, and project management tools.
- **Points of Contact:** Designate primary and secondary points of contact from both sides.
- **Meeting Schedules:** Set up regular meetings to review progress, address issues, and discuss any updates. This may include weekly status meetings, monthly reviews, and ad-hoc meetings as needed.
- **Collaboration Tools:** Utilize collaboration tools to facilitate teamwork and document sharing. Ensure that the third party is familiar with these tools and knows how to use them effectively.

Performance Monitoring and Reporting

Monitoring the performance of the third party is essential to ensure that they meet the agreed-upon standards and deliverables.

- **Key Performance Indicators (KPIs):** Define KPIs to measure the third party's performance. This may include metrics related to quality, timeliness, and customer satisfaction.
- **Reporting Requirements:** Establish reporting requirements for the third party. This may include weekly status reports, monthly performance reviews, and any other relevant updates.
- **Regular Reviews:** Conduct regular performance reviews to assess the third party's progress and address any issues. Use these reviews to provide feedback and discuss any necessary adjustments.
- **Issue Resolution:** Implement a process for identifying and resolving issues promptly. Ensure that the third party knows how to escalate issues and that there is a clear process for addressing them.

Compliance and Regulatory Adherence

Ensuring that the third party complies with relevant regulations and standards is crucial for mitigating risks.

- **Compliance Training:** Provide training to the third party on your organization's compliance requirements and any relevant regulations. This may include training on data protection, industry-specific regulations, and internal policies.
- **Audits and Inspections:** Conduct regular audits and inspections to ensure that the third party adheres to compliance requirements. Use checklists and templates to standardize the audit process.
- **Documentation:** Maintain detailed documentation of the third party's compliance status, including audit reports, training records, and any relevant certifications.
- **Regulatory Updates:** Keep the third party informed about any updates to regulations or standards that may affect their work. Provide guidance on how to implement these updates.

Continual Improvement and Feedback

Encouraging continual improvement and providing regular feedback helps to enhance performance and collaboration with the third party.

- **Feedback Mechanisms:** Implement mechanisms for providing regular feedback to the third party. This may include performance reviews, customer feedback, and internal assessments.
- **Continual Improvement Plans:** Work with the third party to develop continual improvement plans. Identify areas for improvement and set goals for enhancing performance.
- **Training and Development:** Provide opportunities for the third party to enhance their skills and knowledge. This may include training programs, workshops, and access to resources.
- **Recognition and Rewards:** Recognize and reward the third party for outstanding performance. This helps to motivate and encourage them to maintain high standards and also brings in competition and benchmarking between multiple third parties that you may have engaged with.

Conclusion

Effective due diligence and onboarding are critical to establishing successful and risk-free third-party relationships. By following the comprehensive steps outlined in this chapter, you can ensure that your third-party engagements are well-informed, compliant, and beneficial for your organization. Materiality Assessment and Substitutivity Assessment are two vital components that I have devoted full chapter separately on.

Chapter 8: Contracts and Service Level Agreements (SLAs)

In third-party management, Contracts and Service Level Agreements (SLAs) are crucial tools for establishing clear expectations and responsibilities between your organization and the third party. This chapter will delve into the essential elements of these agreements, how to draft them effectively, and provide examples and templates to guide you, because poorly drafted contracts are a risk in managing third parties.

Introduction to Contracts and SLAs

Contracts are formal agreements that outline the terms and conditions of the relationship between your organization and the third party. They provide a legal framework that defines each party's obligations, rights, and remedies in case of a breach. Service Level Agreements (SLAs) are a specific type of contract that focuses on the expected level of service. They set measurable performance standards, outline responsibilities, and detail the consequences of failing to meet these standards.

Key Elements of Contracts and SLAs

Performance metrics are specific criteria used to measure the third party's performance. They should be clear, measurable, and aligned with your organization's objectives. Examples of performance metrics include delivery times (e.g., 95% of deliveries on time), quality standards (e.g., less than 1% defects), and customer satisfaction scores (e.g., average rating above 4.5).

Compliance requirements ensure that the third party adheres to all relevant laws, regulations, and contractual obligations. Examples of compliance requirements include adherence to industry standards (e.g., ISO certifications), compliance with data protection laws (e.g., GDPR), and regular audits and assessments.

Penalties are the consequences outlined in the contract for non-compliance or poor performance. They provide a financial or operational incentive for the third party to meet their obligations. Examples of penalties include financial penalties (e.g., fines for late deliveries), service credits (e.g., free service hours for downtime), and termination clauses (e.g., contract termination for repeated breaches).

Drafting Effective Contracts and SLAs

When drafting contracts and SLAs, it is essential to focus on clarity and precision. Use clear and precise language to avoid ambiguity and define all technical terms and acronyms. Ensure that all performance metrics are quantifiable, including specific targets and acceptable thresholds. Align the contract terms and SLAs with your organizational goals and risk management strategies. Schedule regular reviews of the contract and SLA to ensure they remain relevant and effective and include clauses that allow for adjustments based on changing circumstances or performance reviews.

Always agree two sets of SLAs – one for PEACE time and one for the WAR time!

Example Contracts and SLAs

To help you draft effective contracts and SLAs, here are some examples and templates.

Example 1: Contract Template

Title: [Third-Party Service Contract]

Parties:

- [Your Organization]
- [Third Party]

Scope of Services:

- Detailed description of the services provided by the third party.

Performance Metrics:

- Delivery Timeliness: 95% on-time delivery rate.

- Quality Standards: Less than 1% defect rate.

- Customer Satisfaction: Average rating above 4.5.

Compliance Requirements:

- Adherence to ISO 9001 standards.

- Compliance with GDPR.

- Annual audit requirements.

Penalties:

- Late Delivery: $500 fine per day.

- Service Downtime: 1 hour of free service for every 1 hour of downtime.

- Repeated Breaches: Contract termination after three breaches.

Incentives:

- 1% additional fee for continually meeting the targets for 3 months

Term and Termination:

- Contract term: 12 months.

- Termination clause: Either party can terminate with 30 days' notice.

Signatures:

- [Your Organization Representative]

- [Third Party Representative]

Example 2: SLA Template

Title: [Service Level Agreement]

Parties:

- [Your Organization]

- [Third Party]

Service Scope:

- Description of services covered under the SLA.

Performance Metrics:

- Uptime: 99.9% monthly uptime.

- Response Time: 24-hour response time to critical issues.

- Resolution Time: 48-hour resolution time for critical issues.

Monitoring and Reporting:

- Monthly performance reports.

- Quarterly review meetings.

Penalties:

- Uptime: Service credits for any month below 99.9% uptime.

- Response Time: $100 fine for each incident of delayed response.

- Resolution Time: $200 fine for each incident of delayed resolution.

Review and Revisions:

- Annual review of SLA terms.

- Revisions based on performance and changing requirements.

Signatures:

- [Your Organization Representative]

- [Third Party Representative]

Detailed Guide to Drafting Contracts and SLAs

To draft effective contracts and SLAs, begin by understanding the specific needs and goals of your organization. Determine the critical success factors for the third-party relationship. Clearly outline the scope of services to be provided, including detailed descriptions to avoid misunderstandings. Identify key performance indicators (KPIs) - I will devote a separate chapter to KPIs for Third Parties - relevant to the services and set realistic and achievable targets for each KPI.

List all regulatory and contractual compliance obligations, specifying the frequency and type of audits or assessments required. Outline the penalties for non-compliance or poor performance and include remedies such as service credits or contract termination. Use straightforward language to ensure clarity and avoid legal jargon and ambiguous terms. Involve legal, procurement, and relevant stakeholders in the review process, and ensure all parties understand and agree to the terms. Obtain signatures from authorized representatives of both parties and implement the contract and SLA, beginning regular monitoring.

Third parties pose one of the biggest risks in terms of becoming the insiders. Draft your termination clause extremely carefully to see how you will protect your rights, information, intellectual property.

Conclusion

Contracts and SLAs are essential components of third-party management, providing a clear framework for performance, compliance, and accountability. By carefully drafting and regularly reviewing these agreements, you can ensure that your third-party relationships are effective, compliant, and aligned with your organization's objectives.

Chapter 9: Ongoing Monitoring and Assessment

Introduction to Ongoing Monitoring and Assessment

Ongoing monitoring and assessment of third-party relationships are crucial to ensure that third parties continuously meet compliance, performance, and risk management standards. This chapter explores the techniques and tools used for continuous monitoring and provides detailed guidance on implementing effective monitoring strategies.

Continuous Monitoring Techniques

Continuous monitoring involves regularly assessing third parties to ensure they maintain compliance and performance standards. Effective continuous monitoring techniques include periodic audits, performance reviews, and real-time monitoring.

Periodic Audits are formal examinations of a third party's processes, systems, and operations. They are conducted at regular intervals to verify compliance with regulatory requirements, contractual obligations, and performance standards. Audits can be internal, conducted by your organization, or external, performed by independent auditors. The key objectives of periodic audits include identifying potential risks, verifying the accuracy of reports provided by the third party, and ensuring adherence to agreed-upon standards.

Performance Reviews involve regularly reviewing a third party's performance against agreed-upon metrics and KPIs. These reviews help to ensure that the third party consistently meets performance expectations and allows for the identification and resolution of any performance issues. Performance reviews should be scheduled at regular intervals, such as monthly or quarterly, and should include a thorough analysis of performance data, feedback from stakeholders, and a review of any incidents or issues that have occurred.

Real-Time Monitoring uses technology to continuously monitor third-party activities and performance in real-time. This approach allows for the immediate detection and response to any deviations from expected performance or compliance standards. Real-time monitoring can involve various tools and techniques, such as automated alerts, dashboards, and performance monitoring software. The key benefits of real-time monitoring include the ability to promptly address issues, reduce the risk of compliance breaches, and improve overall third-party performance.

Guidelines to Continuous Monitoring Techniques

To implement effective continuous monitoring, organizations should follow a structured approach that includes planning, execution, and review.

Planning involves defining the scope and objectives of the monitoring program, selecting appropriate monitoring techniques, and establishing monitoring criteria and metrics. Key steps in the planning phase include:

1. Identify Monitoring Objectives:

   o Define the specific goals and objectives of the monitoring program, such as ensuring compliance, assessing performance, or identifying risks.

2. Select Monitoring Techniques:

   o Choose the appropriate monitoring techniques based on the nature of the third-party relationship, the level of risk, and the specific objectives of the monitoring program.

3. Establish Monitoring Criteria:

   o Define the criteria and metrics that will be used to assess third-party performance and compliance. These criteria should be aligned with contractual obligations, regulatory requirements, and organizational objectives.

Execution involves implementing the monitoring techniques, collecting data, and analyzing the results. Key steps in the execution phase include:

1. Conduct Periodic Audits:

   o Schedule and perform regular audits to assess third-party compliance and performance. Use standardized audit checklists and procedures to ensure consistency and thoroughness.

2. Perform Performance Reviews:

   o Regularly review third-party performance against agreed-upon metrics and KPIs. Analyze performance data, gather feedback from stakeholders, and review any incidents or issues.

3. Implement Real-Time Monitoring:

   o Use technology tools to continuously monitor third-party activities and performance in real-time. Set up automated alerts and dashboards to promptly detect and respond to any deviations from expected performance or compliance standards.

Review involves evaluating the effectiveness of the monitoring program, identifying areas for improvement, and making necessary adjustments. Key steps in the review phase include:

1. Evaluate Monitoring Results:

   o Review the results of audits, performance reviews, and real-time monitoring to assess the overall effectiveness of the monitoring program. Identify any trends, patterns, or recurring issues.

2. Identify Areas for Improvement:

   o Determine areas where the monitoring program can be enhanced, such as improving audit procedures, refining performance metrics, or upgrading monitoring technology.

3. Make Adjustments:

   o Implement necessary changes to the monitoring program based on the evaluation results. Continuously update monitoring techniques and criteria to ensure they remain relevant and effective.

Tools and Examples for Continuous Monitoring

Various tools and technologies can be used to support continuous monitoring efforts. These tools include audit management software, performance management systems, and real-time monitoring platforms.

Audit Management Software helps streamline the audit process by providing standardized checklists, automated workflows, and reporting capabilities. Examples of audit management software include AuditBoard, MetricStream, and TeamMate.

Performance Management Systems enable organizations to track and analyze third-party performance data. These systems provide dashboards, performance reports, and analytics tools to help identify trends and areas for improvement. Examples of performance management systems include SAP SuccessFactors, Oracle HCM, and Workday.

Real-Time Monitoring Platforms provide real-time visibility into third-party activities and performance. These platforms offer automated alerts, dashboards, and analytics to help organizations promptly detect and address any issues. Examples of real-time monitoring platforms include Splunk, Dynatrace, and New Relic.

Conclusion

Ongoing monitoring and assessment are essential for ensuring that third parties consistently meet compliance, performance, and risk management standards. By implementing effective continuous monitoring techniques, such as periodic audits, performance reviews, and real-time monitoring, organizations can promptly detect and address any issues, reduce risks, and enhance overall third-party performance. This chapter has provided a comprehensive guide to continuous monitoring techniques, including tools and examples, to help organizations establish and maintain effective monitoring programs. I will cover KPIs in the next chapter.

This appears to be a big game and hence my recommendation is to introduce a new role – the CVDM (Chief Vendor Data Manager)!

Chapter 10: Key Performance Indicators (KPIs) for Third Parties

Introduction to KPIs for Third Parties

Key Performance Indicators (KPIs) are critical metrics used to measure and evaluate the performance of third-party service providers, including those supplying products, services or raw materials. Establishing clear KPIs ensures that third parties meet performance, compliance, and strategic objectives. This chapter provides a comprehensive guide to developing and implementing KPIs for third parties, focusing on those providing raw materials.

Importance of KPIs in Third-Party Management

KPIs are crucial in third-party management for the following reasons:

1. **Aligning Objectives:** Ensuring third-party activities align with organizational goals.

2. **Improving Performance:** Identifying areas for improvement and driving continuous improvement.

3. **Enhancing Accountability:** Establishing clear performance expectations and accountability.

4. **Managing Risks:** Identifying potential risks and implementing corrective actions.

5. **Facilitating Decision-Making:** Providing data-driven insights for informed decision-making.

Developing Effective KPIs

To develop effective KPIs, organizations should follow these steps:

1. **Define Objectives:** Identify the specific objectives you want to achieve with your third-party relationships.

2. **Select Relevant KPIs:** Choose KPIs that are directly aligned with these objectives and relevant to the third party's role.

3. **Set Targets:** Establish clear and achievable targets for each KPI.

4. **Ensure Measurability:** Ensure that each KPI is quantifiable and can be measured accurately.

5. **Communicate Expectations:** Clearly communicate KPI expectations to the third party. This could have been done in the contract.

6. **Review and Adjust:** Regularly review KPI performance and adjust targets as necessary.

Categories of KPIs for Raw Materials

KPIs for third parties providing raw materials can be categorized into several key areas, including quality, delivery, cost, compliance, and relationship management. Each category addresses different aspects of third-party performance and risk management.

Quality KPIs:

- **Material Quality:** Measures the quality of raw materials supplied.

- **Defect Rate:** Assesses the rate of defects in the raw materials.

- **Consistency:** Evaluates the consistency of material properties batch-to-batch.

Delivery KPIs:

- **On-Time Delivery:** Measures the percentage of deliveries made on time.

- **Lead Time:** Assesses the time taken from order placement to delivery.

- **Order Accuracy:** Evaluates the accuracy of orders fulfilled by the third party.

Cost KPIs:

- **Cost Efficiency:** Measures the cost-effectiveness of the raw materials supplied.

- **Price Stability:** Assesses the stability of raw material prices over time.

- **Total Cost of Ownership:** Evaluates the overall cost, including purchase price, transportation, and handling.

Compliance KPIs:

- **Regulatory Compliance:** Evaluates adherence to relevant laws and regulations.

- **Supplier Certifications:** Assesses the validity and currency of necessary certifications.

- **Audit Results:** Measures the outcomes of periodic audits and compliance assessments.

Relationship Management KPIs:

- **Communication Effectiveness:** Measures the quality and timeliness of communication between the parties.

- **Issue Resolution:** Assesses the third party's ability to resolve issues promptly and effectively.

- **Collaboration and Partnership:** Evaluates the strength of the collaborative relationship.

Suggested KPIs, Definitions, Weightages, and Scoring

Below are suggested KPIs for each category, along with their definitions, weightages, and scoring methodologies.

Quality KPIs:

1. **Material Quality**

   - **Definition:** The quality of raw materials supplied, based on industry standards and specifications.

   - **Weightage:** 7%

   - **Scoring:**

     - 100% compliance with quality standards: 5 points
     - 95-99% compliance: 4 points
     - 90-94% compliance: 3 points
     - 85-89% compliance: 2 points
     - Below 85% compliance: 1 point

2. **Defect Rate**

   - **Definition:** The rate of defects in the raw materials supplied.

   - **Weightage:** 5%

   - **Scoring:**

     - Less than 1% defects: 5 points
     - 1-2% defects: 4 points

- 2-3% defects: 3 points
- 3-4% defects: 2 points
- Above 4% defects: 1 point

3. **Consistency**

   o **Definition:** Consistency of material properties batch-to-batch.

   o **Weightage:** 7%

   o **Scoring:**

     - Highly consistent: 5 points
     - Consistent: 4 points
     - Moderately consistent: 3 points
     - Inconsistent: 2 points
     - Highly inconsistent: 1 point

Delivery KPIs:

4. **On-Time Delivery**

   o **Definition:** Percentage of deliveries made on time.

   o **Weightage:** 5%

   o **Scoring:**

     - 95-100% on-time: 5 points
     - 90-94% on-time: 4 points
     - 85-89% on-time: 3 points
     - 80-84% on-time: 2 points
     - Below 80% on-time: 1 point

5. **Lead Time**

   o **Definition:** Time taken from order placement to delivery.

   o **Weightage:** 5%

   o **Scoring:**

     - Lead time < 1 week: 5 points
     - Lead time 1-2 weeks: 4 points
     - Lead time 2-3 weeks: 3 points
     - Lead time 3-4 weeks: 2 points
     - Lead time > 4 weeks: 1 point

6. **Order Accuracy**

   o **Definition:** Accuracy of fulfilled orders compared to order specifications.

   o **Weightage:** 7%

   o **Scoring:**

     - 99-100% accurate: 5 points
     - 97-98% accurate: 4 points
     - 95-96% accurate: 3 points
     - 93-94% accurate: 2 points
     - Below 93% accurate: 1 point

Cost KPIs:

7. **Cost Efficiency**

   o **Definition:** Cost-effectiveness of raw materials supplied.

- o **Weightage:** 7%

- o **Scoring:**

    - Costs < 90% of budget: 5 points
    - Costs 90-100% of budget: 4 points
    - Costs 100-110% of budget: 3 points
    - Costs 110-120% of budget: 2 points
    - Costs > 120% of budget: 1 point

8. **Price Stability**

    - o **Definition:** Stability of raw material prices over time.

    - o **Weightage:** 5%

    - o **Scoring:**

        - Prices stable with less than 2% variation: 5 points
        - Prices with 2-4% variation: 4 points
        - Prices with 4-6% variation: 3 points
        - Prices with 6-8% variation: 2 points
        - Prices with more than 8% variation: 1 point

9. **Total Cost of Ownership**

    - o **Definition:** Overall cost including purchase price, transportation, and handling.

    - o **Weightage:** 7%

    - o **Scoring:**

        - TCO < 90% of budget: 5 points
        - TCO 90-100% of budget: 4 points
        - TCO 100-110% of budget: 3 points
        - TCO 110-120% of budget: 2 points
        - TCO > 120% of budget: 1 point

Compliance KPIs:

10. **Regulatory Compliance**

    - o **Definition:** Adherence to relevant laws and regulations.

    - o **Weightage:** 7%

    - o **Scoring:**

        - 100% compliance: 5 points
        - 90-99% compliance: 4 points
        - 80-89% compliance: 3 points
        - 70-79% compliance: 2 points
        - Below 70% compliance: 1 point

11. **Supplier Certifications**

    - o **Definition:** Validity and currency of necessary certifications.

    - o **Weightage:** 5%

    - o **Scoring:**

        - All required certifications up to date: 5 points
        - 1 certification expiring within 3 months: 4 points
        - 2 certifications expiring within 3 months: 3 points
        - 3 certifications expiring within 3 months: 2 points
        - More than 3 certifications expiring within 3 months: 1 point

12. **Audit Results**

   o **Definition:** Outcomes of periodic audits and compliance assessments.

   o **Weightage:** 5%

   o **Scoring:**

      - No findings: 5 points
      - Minor findings: 4 points
      - Moderate findings: 3 points
      - Significant findings: 2 points
      - Major findings: 1 point

Relationship Management KPIs:

13. **Communication Effectiveness**

   o **Definition:** Quality and timeliness of communication.

   o **Weightage:** 5%

   o **Scoring:**

      - Excellent communication: 5 points
      - Good communication: 4 points
      - Average communication: 3 points
      - Below average communication: 2 points
      - Poor communication: 1 point

14. **Issue Resolution**

   o **Definition: Ability to resolve issues promptly.**

   o **Weightage: 5%**

   o **Scoring:**

      - Issues resolved within 24 hours: 5 points
      - Issues resolved within 48 hours: 4 points
      - Issues resolved within 72 hours: 3 points
      - Issues resolved within a week: 2 points
      - Issues unresolved for more than a week: 1 point

15. **Collaboration and Partnership**

   o **Definition:** Strength of the collaborative relationship.

   o **Weightage:** 5%

   o **Scoring:**

      - Highly collaborative: 5 points
      - Collaborative: 4 points
      - Moderately collaborative: 3 points
      - Less collaborative: 2 points
      - Not collaborative: 1 point

New Possibilities KPIs:

16. **Innovation and R&D**

   o **Definition:** Investment in innovation and R&D and achievements.

   o **Weightage:** 7%

   o **Scoring:**

- Highly innovative/ >15% of revenues invested in R&D/ many patents: 5 points
- Innovative/ up to 10% of revenues invested in R&D/ some patents: 4 points
- Moderately Innovative/ up to 5% of revenues invested in R&D/ few patents: 3 points
- Less Innovative/ up to 2% of revenues invested in R&D/ some patents filed: 2 points
- Not Innovative/ no investment in R&D, no patents: 1 point

17. **Capability/ capacity to do/ provide more/ quick ramp up**

- o **Definition:** Capacity and capability to provide additional products/ services.

- o **Weightage:** 6%

- o **Scoring:**

  - High capacity/ free capacity/ commitment and availability of funds to invest: 5 points
  - Moderate capacity, commitment and availability of funds to invest: 4 points
  - Low capacity, commitment and availability of funds to invest: 3 points
  - Less capacity, commitment and availability of funds to invest: 2 points
  - Capacity full, non-availability of funds to invest: 1 point

Sample Score Card

Category	KPI	Score (1-5)	Weightage (%)	Weighted Score	Scoring Guideline
Quality KPIs	Material Quality	5	7%	0.35	100% compliance with quality standards: 5 points 95-99% compliance: 4 points 90-94% compliance: 3 points 85-89% compliance: 2 points Below 85% compliance: 1 point
	Defect Rate	5	5%	0.25	Less than 1% defects: 5 points 1-2% defects: 4 points 2-3% defects: 3 points 3-4% defects: 2 points Above 4% defects: 1 point
	Consistency	5	7%	0.35	Highly consistent: 5 points Consistent: 4 points Moderately consistent: 3 points Inconsistent: 2 points Highly inconsistent: 1 point
Delivery KPIs	On-Time Delivery	5	5%	0.25	95-100% on-time: 5 points 90-94% on-time: 4 points 85-89% on-time: 3 points 80-84% on-time: 2 points Below 80% on-time: 1 point
Delivery KPIs	Lead Time	5	5%	0.25	Lead time < 1 week: 5 points Lead time 1-2 weeks: 4 points Lead time 2-3 weeks: 3 points Lead time 3-4 weeks: 2 points Lead time > 4 weeks: 1 point
	Order Accuracy	5	7%	0.35	99-100% accurate: 5 points 97-98% accurate: 4 points 95-96% accurate: 3 points 93-94% accurate: 2 points Below 93% accurate: 1 point

Category	KPI	Score (1-5)	Weightage (%)	Weighted Score	Scoring Guideline
Cost KPIs	Cost Efficiency	5	7%	0.35	Costs < 90% of budget: 5 points Costs 90-100% of budget: 4 points Costs 100-110% of budget: 3 points Costs 110-120% of budget: 2 points Costs > 120% of budget: 1 point
	Price Stability	5	5%	0.25	Prices stable with less than 2% variation: 5 points Prices with 2-4% variation: 4 points Prices with 4-6% variation: 3 points Prices with 6-8% variation: 2 points Prices with more than 8% variation: 1 point
	Total Cost of Ownership	5	7%	0.35	TCO < 90% of budget: 5 points TCO 90-100% of budget: 4 points TCO 100-110% of budget: 3 points TCO 110-120% of budget: 2 points TCO > 120% of budget: 1 point
Compliance KPIs	Regulatory Compliance	5	7%	0.35	100% compliance: 5 points 90-99% compliance: 4 points 80-89% compliance: 3 points 70-79% compliance: 2 points Below 70% compliance: 1 point
	Supplier Certifications	5	5%	0.25	All required certifications up to date: 5 points 1 certification expiring within 3 months: 4 points 2 certifications expiring within 3 months: 3 points 3 certifications expiring within 3 months: 2 points More than 3 certifications expiring within 3 months: 1 point
	Audit Results	5	5%	0.25	No findings: 5 points Minor findings: 4 points Moderate findings: 3 points Significant findings: 2 points Major findings: 1 point
Relationship Management KPIs:	Communication Effectiveness	5	5%	0.25	Excellent communication: 5 points Good communication: 4 points Average communication: 3 points Below average communication: 2 points Poor communication: 1 point

Category	KPI	Score (1-5)	Weightage (%)	Weighted Score	Scoring Guideline
	Issue Resolution	5	5%	0.25	Issues resolved within 24 hours: 5 points Issues resolved within 48 hours: 4 points Issues resolved within 72 hours: 3 points Issues resolved within a week: 2 points Issues unresolved for more than a week: 1 point
	Collaboration and Partnership	5	5%	0.25	Highly collaborative: 5 points Collaborative: 4 points Moderately collaborative: 3 points Less collaborative: 2 points Not collaborative: 1 point
New Possibilities KPIs	Innovation and R&D	5	7%	0.35	Highly innovative/ >15% of revenues invested in R&D/ many patents: 5 points Innovative/ up to 10% of revenues invested in R&D/ some patents: 4 points Moderately Innovative/ up to 5% of revenues invested in R&D/ few patents: 3 points Less Innovative/ up to 2% of revenues invested in R&D/ some patents filed: 2 points Not Innovative/ no investment in R&D, no patents: 0 point
	Capability/ capacity to do/ provide more/ quick ramp up	5	6%	0.3	High capacity/ free capacity/ commitment and availability of funds to invest: 5 points Moderate capacity, commitment and availability of funds to invest: 4 points Low capacity, commitment and availability of funds to invest: 3 points Less capacity, commitment and availability of funds to invest: 2 points Capacity full, non availability of funds to invest: 1 point
Total			100%	5	

Implementing and Managing KPIs

To effectively implement and manage KPIs, organizations should follow these steps:

1. **Communicate KPIs:** Ensure that third parties understand the KPIs, their importance, and how they will be measured.

2. **Collect Data:** Establish systems and processes for collecting and analyzing performance data.

3. **Review Performance:** Regularly review KPI performance with third parties, identifying areas for improvement and recognizing achievements.

4. **Adjust KPIs:** Continuously evaluate and adjust KPIs to ensure they remain relevant and aligned with organizational goals.

5. **Use Technology:** Leverage technology tools to automate data collection, analysis, and reporting of KPIs.

KPI Tracking Dashboard: A dashboard tool that allows real-time tracking and visualization of KPI performance, facilitating data-driven decision-making and timely interventions.

Automated Reporting Tool: Software that automates the collection, analysis, and reporting of KPI data, ensuring accuracy and efficiency in performance monitoring.

Conclusion

Implementing KPIs for third-party management, especially for raw material suppliers, is essential for ensuring quality, timely delivery, cost efficiency, and strong collaborative relationships. By following the steps outlined in this chapter and utilizing the provided templates and tools, organizations can establish a robust KPI framework that drives performance improvements, manages risks, and supports strategic objectives.

Chapter 11: The TPRM Cycle

Here is my TPRM Lifecycle:

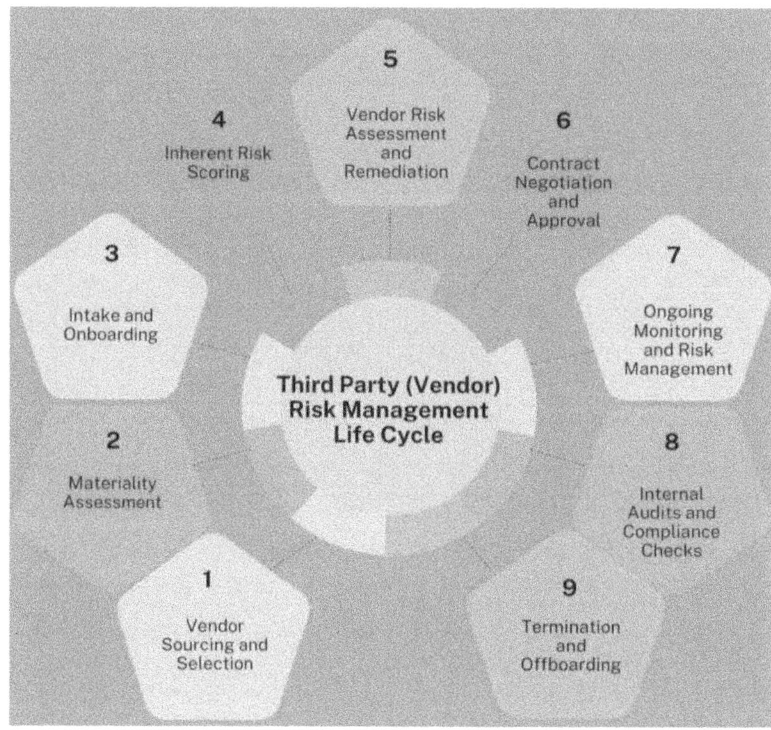

1. Vendor Sourcing and Selection

In this phase, the organization identifies potential vendors that could fulfill their specific needs. This process involves extensive research, networking, and possibly utilizing vendor databases or industry directories. Critical activities include:

- **Defining Requirements**: Clearly outline the services or products needed, including any specific criteria like compliance with certain standards, geographic location, or technological capabilities.
- **Market Research**: Conduct market analysis to identify potential vendors, considering factors such as market share, reputation, and past performance.
- **Preliminary Materiality Assessment**: Conduct an initial assessment to determine which vendors are most likely to have a significant impact on the organization based on factors such as size, scope of services, and criticality to operations.
- **Request for Proposal (RFP)**: Develop and distribute an RFP to gather detailed information from potential vendors, including their qualifications, experience, and proposed solutions.

2. Materiality Assessment

Materiality assessment is a systematic process to evaluate the significance of each vendor to the organization. This step helps prioritize resources and focus on vendors that pose the greatest potential risk or have the most significant impact. Key activities include:

- **Criteria Development**: Establish criteria for assessing materiality, such as financial impact, operational dependency, compliance requirements, and strategic importance.
- **Vendor Evaluation**: Assess each vendor against these criteria using qualitative and quantitative methods.

- **Scoring and Ranking**: Assign scores to each vendor based on their materiality, creating a ranking that highlights the most critical vendors.
- **Documentation and Reporting**: Document the assessment process and results, providing a clear rationale for the prioritization of vendors.

3. Intake and Onboarding

Once a vendor is selected, the onboarding process ensures they are integrated into the organization's systems and processes efficiently and effectively. This phase includes:

- **Contract Finalization**: Finalize the contract terms, ensuring all necessary clauses related to compliance, performance, and risk management are included.
- **Orientation and Training**: Provide training and orientation to the vendor on the organization's policies, procedures, and expectations.
- **System Integration**: Integrate the vendor's systems with the organization's IT infrastructure, ensuring secure and seamless data exchange.
- **Initial Risk Assessment**: Conduct an initial risk assessment focusing on the materiality of the vendor to identify any immediate risks that need to be addressed during onboarding.

4. Inherent Risk Scoring

Inherent risk scoring assesses the baseline risk associated with each vendor based on the nature of their services and the context of their engagement. Activities include:

- **Risk Identification**: Identify potential risks related to the vendor, such as data security, financial stability, operational reliability, and compliance with regulations.
- **Risk Assessment Tools**: Utilize risk assessment tools and methodologies to evaluate inherent risks, such as risk matrices, checklists, and scoring models.
- **Scoring Criteria**: Develop criteria for scoring inherent risks, taking into account factors like the sensitivity of data handled, criticality of services provided, and potential regulatory impact.
- **Risk Scoring**: Assign scores to each vendor based on the identified risks, providing a baseline for further risk management activities.

5. Vendor Risk Assessment and Remediation

This phase involves conducting detailed risk assessments to identify specific vulnerabilities and developing remediation plans to address them. Key activities include:

- **Detailed Risk Assessments**: Perform in-depth assessments of vendor risks, including security audits, financial reviews, and compliance checks.
- **Risk Mitigation Plans**: Develop and implement plans to mitigate identified risks, such as improving security controls, enhancing financial monitoring, or renegotiating contract terms.
- **Remediation Tracking**: Track the progress of remediation efforts, ensuring that identified risks are addressed promptly and effectively.
- **Vendor Communication**: Maintain open communication with vendors throughout the remediation process to ensure they understand and comply with the necessary risk mitigation measures.

6. Contract Negotiation and Approval

Negotiating and finalizing contracts with vendors is crucial to ensuring that all risk management concerns are adequately addressed. This phase includes:

- **Contract Drafting**: Draft contract terms that clearly outline the expectations, responsibilities, and obligations of both parties.

- **Risk Clauses**: Include specific clauses related to risk management, such as data protection, performance monitoring, compliance requirements, and termination conditions.
- **Negotiation**: Engage in negotiations with vendors to reach mutually agreeable terms that protect the organization's interests.
- **Approval Process**: Obtain necessary internal approvals for the contract, ensuring all relevant stakeholders have reviewed and endorsed the terms.

7. Ongoing Monitoring and Risk Management

Continuous monitoring of vendor performance and risk exposure is essential to maintaining a robust TPRM program. Key activities include:

- **Performance Metrics**: Establish performance metrics and key performance indicators (KPIs) to monitor vendor performance regularly.
- **Regular Assessments**: Conduct regular risk assessments and reviews to identify any changes in risk exposure or performance issues.
- **Real-time Monitoring**: Utilize real-time monitoring tools and technologies to detect potential issues promptly, such as security incidents or operational disruptions.
- **Feedback Mechanisms**: Implement feedback mechanisms to gather input from internal stakeholders and the vendor regarding performance and risk management.

8. Internal Audits and Compliance Checks

Periodic internal audits and compliance checks ensure that vendors adhere to contractual obligations and regulatory requirements. This phase includes:

- **Audit Planning**: Develop an audit plan that outlines the scope, objectives, and schedule for auditing vendor relationships.
- **Compliance Checks**: Conduct compliance checks to verify that vendors meet all contractual and regulatory requirements.
- **Audit Execution**: Perform audits according to the plan, using a combination of document reviews, interviews, and on-site inspections.
- **Reporting and Follow-up**: Document audit findings and recommendations and follow up with vendors to ensure corrective actions are implemented.

9. Termination and Offboarding

Managing the termination of vendor relationships is critical to ensuring a smooth transition and mitigating any residual risks. Key activities include:

- **Termination Planning**: Develop a plan for terminating the vendor relationship, including timelines, responsibilities, and communication strategies.
- **Data Transfer and Security**: Ensure the secure transfer or destruction of data held by the vendor, in accordance with contractual and regulatory requirements.
- **Contract Closure**: Close out all contractual obligations, including final payments, return of assets, and resolution of any outstanding issues.
- **Post-Termination Review**: Conduct a post-termination review to evaluate the overall relationship and identify any lessons learned for future vendor engagements.

Conclusion

A comprehensive Third Party Risk Management (TPRM) cycle ensures that organizations effectively manage their vendor relationships, mitigate risks, and maintain compliance with regulatory requirements. By incorporating a materiality assessment, organizations can prioritize their efforts and focus on managing the most critical vendors. This approach not only enhances risk management but also strengthens overall vendor performance and organizational resilience.

Chapter 12: Materiality Assessment and Substitutivity Assessment

Materiality Assessment and Substitutivity Assessment are so important but least understood terms and steps in TPRM that I thought of devoting a chapter on these.

Materiality Assessment in TPRM

Materiality assessment in TPRM is a process used to identify and prioritize third-party entities, including vendors, suppliers, partners, and contractors, that are most critical to an organization. This helps in focusing risk management efforts on the most significant relationships, ensuring that key third parties are monitored and managed effectively to mitigate potential risks.

Steps Involved:

1. **Identification of Third Parties:**
   o Compile a comprehensive list of all third-party entities, including vendors, suppliers, partners, and contractors.
2. **Assessment Criteria Development:**
   o Develop criteria to evaluate the significance of each third party. This may include factors such as the volume of business, financial impact, operational dependency, regulatory requirements, and reputational risk.
3. **Stakeholder Engagement:**
   o Engage with internal stakeholders (e.g., procurement, finance, operations, legal) to gather insights on which third parties are most critical to the organization's operations and objectives.
4. **Assessment and Prioritization:**
   o Evaluate each third party against the developed criteria to determine their materiality. Rank them based on their importance and the potential impact on the organization.
5. **Validation and Review:**
   o Validate the findings with senior management and relevant departments. Review and update the materiality assessment periodically to ensure it remains relevant as business conditions and third-party relationships evolve.

Relation to TPRM:

- **Risk Identification:**
  o Materiality assessment helps identify key third-party relationships that pose significant risks to the organization, allowing for targeted risk management efforts.
- **Prioritization:**
  o Ensures that TPRM resources are focused on managing risks associated with the most critical third parties, aligning with the organization's risk management strategy.
- **Stakeholder Alignment:**
  o Involving stakeholders in the materiality assessment process ensures that third-party risks are evaluated in line with business objectives and stakeholder concerns.

Stage Conducted:

Materiality assessments in TPRM are typically conducted during the initial phases of the TPRM program setup and revisited periodically (e.g., annually) to ensure ongoing relevance and to adapt to any changes in third-party relationships or business conditions.

Here I produce a sample scoring criteria for Materiality Assessment:

Assessment Criteria Development

1. **Volume of Business**
   - **Description:** The extent of business conducted with the third party.
   - **Scoring:** High volume = High score.
   - **Weight:** High weight if business volume significantly impacts the organization.

2. **Financial Impact**
   - **Description:** The financial consequences of the relationship with the third party.
   - **Scoring:** High financial impact = High score.
   - **Weight:** High weight if the financial impact is critical to the organization's operations.

3. **Operational Dependency**
   - **Description:** The degree to which the organization relies on the third party for its operations.
   - **Scoring:** High dependency = High score.
   - **Weight:** High weight if the dependency affects core operations.

4. **Regulatory Requirements**
   - **Description:** The importance of the third party in meeting regulatory compliance.
   - **Scoring:** High regulatory impact = High score.
   - **Weight:** High weight if regulatory compliance is crucial.

5. **Reputational Risk**
   - **Description:** The potential impact on the organization's reputation due to the third party's actions or failures.
   - **Scoring:** High reputational risk = High score.
   - **Weight:** High weight if reputational damage could significantly impact the organization.

6. **Quality of Service**
   - **Description:** Importance of the quality and reliability of the services provided by the third party.
   - **Scoring:** High quality risk = High score.
   - **Weight:** High weight if poor service quality hits business operations badly.

7. **Geopolitical Risk**
   - **Description:** The risk associated with the third party's geographical location.
   - **Scoring:** High geopolitical risk = High score.
   - **Weight:** High weight if geopolitical instability could affect the third party's performance.
   - **Innovation Capability**
   - **Description:** The ability of the third party to innovate and adapt to changing business needs.
   - **Scoring:** High innovation risk = High score.
   - **Weight:** High weight if innovation is crucial for competitive advantage.

Sample Scoring Sheet

Criteria	Description	Score Range	Weight	Weighted Score
Volume of Business	Extent of business conducted	1-5	20%	
Financial Impact	Financial consequences of the relationship	1-5	20%	
Operational Dependency	Reliance on third party for operations	1-5	20%	
Regulatory Requirements	Importance in meeting compliance	1-5	15%	
Reputational Risk	Potential impact on reputation	1-5	15%	
Quality of Service	Quality and reliability of services	1-5	5%	
Geopolitical Risk	Risk associated with geographical location	1-5	3%	
Innovation Capability	Ability to innovate and adapt	1-5	2%	

Scoring Guide

- **1:** Low impact/significance
- **2:** Moderate impact/significance
- **3:** Considerable impact/significance
- **4:** High impact/significance
- **5:** Critical impact/significance

Calculation of Weighted Score

For each criterion, multiply the score by the weight to get the weighted score. Sum all weighted scores to get the total score for each third party.

Example Calculation

Criteria	Score	Weight	Weighted Score
Volume of Business	4	20%	0.8
Financial Impact	5	20%	1
Operational Dependency	3	20%	0.6
Regulatory Requirements	2	15%	0.3
Reputational Risk	5	15%	0.75
Quality of Service	3	5%	0.15
Geopolitical Risk	4	3%	0.12
Innovation Capability	3	2%	0.06

Total Weighted Score: 0.8 + 1.0 + 0.6 + 0.3 + 0.75 + 0.15 + 0.12 + 0.06 = 3.78

Using this approach, you can systematically evaluate and prioritize third-party entities based on their significance to your organization, focusing your TPRM efforts on managing the most critical relationships.

In this case the highest value is 5 i.e. the third party has the highest materiality or super critical third party of the organization is acutely dependent on this third party.

Similarly, the lowest value is 1 i.e. the third party provides the least important services to the organization.

Substitutivity Assessment in TPRM

Substitutivity assessment evaluates the ability to replace a particular supplier, product, or service with an alternative in case of disruption. It assesses the availability, cost, and feasibility of substitutes, aiming to ensure business continuity and minimize risk.

Steps Involved:

1. **Identification of Critical Suppliers**: Identify suppliers and services that are critical to operations. Materiality Assessment could be used here.
2. **Assessment of Alternatives**: Evaluate the availability of alternative suppliers or services and their ability to meet requirements.
3. **Feasibility Analysis**: Assess the feasibility of switching to alternatives, considering factors such as cost, quality, and lead times.
4. **Implementation Planning**: Develop plans for how to switch to alternatives in case of disruption.

Relation to TPRM:

- **Resilience Planning**: Substitutivity assessment is a key component of resilience planning, ensuring that the organization can continue operations despite third-party disruptions.
- **Risk Mitigation**: It helps mitigate risks associated with dependency on single suppliers or critical services.

- **Decision Making**: Provides data for informed decision-making about supplier relationships and diversification strategies.

Stage Conducted: Substitutivity assessments are typically conducted as part of the risk management and business continuity planning processes. They may be revisited regularly or when there are significant changes in the supply chain or market conditions.

Integration with TPRM

Materiality Assessment in TPRM:

- **Initial Risk Assessment**: Conduct materiality assessments during the initial risk assessment phase of TPRM to identify and prioritize key risks.
- **Ongoing Monitoring**: Use the findings from materiality assessments to continuously monitor and reassess third-party risks.

Substitutivity Assessment in TPRM:

- **Risk Mitigation Planning**: Perform substitutivity assessments as part of the risk mitigation planning within TPRM to ensure alternatives are available and viable.
- **Business Continuity**: Integrate substitutivity assessments into business continuity plans to prepare for potential disruptions in the supply chain.

Both assessments are crucial for effective TPRM, providing a comprehensive understanding of risks and ensuring preparedness for managing third-party disruptions.

Assume a third party has been scored high on Materiality Assessment. Now a Substitutivity Assessment needs to be conducted for this third party i.e. whether the organization can substitute this third party with an alternative.

Here is my proposed list of parameters for Substitutivity Assessment.

1. **Third Party Evaluation**
   o **Supplier Availability**: Number of alternative third parties available.
   o **Supplier Reliability**: Track record of reliability and performance.
   o **Supplier Capacity**: Ability to meet required volumes and demand.
   o **Supplier Location**: Geographic proximity and impact on logistics.

2. **Product/Service Evaluation**

   o **Quality Match**: Compatibility with current quality standards and specifications.
   o **Technical Compatibility**: Technical feasibility of integration with existing systems.
   o **Lead Time**: Time required to source and receive products/services.
   o **Cost Impact**: Comparison of costs with primary supplier, including any switching costs.

These parameters are for the existing third party and help to decide whether this can be substituted or not. If the overall score comes out to be low (1 is lowest) then the answer is NO, while with a higher score (5 is maximum), another third party must be located as soon as possible.

The following parameters will then help establish whether the new party can substitute the existing one, or if more than one new party are available then which one should be picked up (the one with high score)

1. **Operational Impact**
   o **Implementation Feasibility**: Ease of transitioning to the alternative party.
   o **Training Requirements**: Need for training or re-skilling employees.
   o **Disruption Risk**: Potential operational disruptions during the switch.
   o **Compliance Requirements**: Adherence to regulatory and compliance requirements.

2. **Financial Impact**

   o **Cost Efficiency**: Cost savings or increases from using the alternative party.
   o **Financial Stability**: Financial health and stability of the alternative party.
   o **Investment Needs**: Any capital investments required for the switch.
   o **Return on Investment**: Long-term financial benefits compared to initial costs.

3. **Strategic Alignment**

   o **Business Strategy Fit**: Alignment with overall business strategy and goals.
   o **Risk Mitigation**: Contribution to overall risk mitigation strategies.

Scoring Sheet Template

(for existing party)

Parameter	Score (1-5)	Weight	Weighted Score (Score x Weight)
Supplier Availability	5	15%	0.75
Supplier Reliability	5	15%	0.75
Supplier Capacity	5	15%	0.75
Supplier Location	5	10%	0.5
Quality Match	5	10%	0.5
Technical Compatibility	5	10%	0.5
Lead Time	5	10%	0.5
Cost Impact	5	15%	0.75

Sample score = 5

(for new party)

Parameter	Score (1-5)	Weight	Weighted Score (Score x Weight)
Implementation Feasibility	5	15%	0.75
Training Requirements	1	10%	0.1
Disruption Risk	1	10%	0.1

Parameter	Score (1-5)	Weight	Weighted Score (Score x Weight)
Compliance Requirements	1	10%	0.1
Cost Efficiency	5	15%	0.75
Financial Stability	5	10%	0.5
Investment Needs	1	10%	0.1
Return on Investment	5	5%	0.25
Business Strategy Fit	5	5%	0.25
Risk Mitigation	5	10%	0.5

A score of 3.4 for the new party is ideal for switching.

A risk should be recorded in both cases:

    a) If the Substitutivity assessment for existing party is low (it may become a single point of failure).
    b) If the substitutivity assessment for a new party is low.

Materiality Assessment Process

The materiality assessment process is a systematic approach to evaluate and prioritize vendors based on their significance and potential impact on the organization. This process helps organizations focus their risk management efforts on the most critical vendor relationships. Here is a detailed description of the materiality assessment process:

1. Define Objectives and Scope

Objective Setting

- Determine the goals of the materiality assessment, such as identifying high-risk vendors, prioritizing resources, or ensuring compliance.
- Define the key outcomes expected from the assessment.

Scope Definition

- Identify the categories of vendors to be assessed, such as IT services, manufacturing, or logistics.
- Determine the timeframe for the assessment and the frequency of updates (e.g., annually, semi-annually).

2. Develop Assessment Criteria

Criteria Selection

- Choose criteria that are relevant to your organization's context and risk appetite. Common criteria include financial impact, operational dependence, data sensitivity, regulatory compliance, and reputational risk.

Weighting Criteria

- Assign weights to each criterion based on its importance to the organization. For example, data sensitivity might be weighted higher for a technology company.

3. Data Collection

Internal Data Gathering

- Collect internal data on vendors, such as contract details, performance metrics, financial transactions, and incident reports.

External Data Gathering

- Obtain external data from sources like credit ratings, industry reports, regulatory filings, and news articles.

Vendor Questionnaires

- Distribute questionnaires to vendors to gather specific information on their operations, financial health, security practices, and compliance status.

4. Vendor Evaluation

Score Calculation

- Evaluate each vendor against the defined criteria, using a scoring system to quantify their materiality. Scores can be numerical (e.g., 1 to 5) or categorical (e.g., low, medium, high).

Data Analysis

- Analyze the collected data to identify patterns, outliers, and trends. Use statistical methods and data visualization tools to support the analysis.

5. Risk Ranking and Prioritization

Vendor Ranking

- Rank vendors based on their overall materiality scores, from highest to lowest.

Risk Prioritization

- Prioritize vendors that require immediate attention due to high scores in critical criteria, such as financial impact or data sensitivity.

6. Reporting and Documentation

Report Preparation

- Prepare detailed reports on the materiality assessment findings, including the criteria used, scores assigned, and rationale for prioritization.

Stakeholder Communication

- Share the assessment results with relevant stakeholders, such as senior management, risk management teams, and procurement departments.

Documentation

- Document the assessment process, data sources, scoring methodology, and findings for future reference and audit purposes.

7. Action Planning

Risk Mitigation Plans

- Develop risk mitigation plans for high-priority vendors, addressing identified vulnerabilities and compliance gaps.

Resource Allocation

- Allocate resources and assign responsibilities for managing high-materiality vendors, including regular monitoring and periodic reviews.

8. Continuous Monitoring and Review

Ongoing Monitoring

- Continuously monitor high-materiality vendors using predefined metrics and performance indicators. Implement real-time monitoring tools where possible.

Periodic Reviews

- Conduct periodic reviews of the materiality assessment to ensure it remains relevant and up to date. Adjust criteria, weights, and scoring as needed.

Feedback Loop

- Establish a feedback loop to incorporate lessons learned and improve the assessment process over time. Gather input from stakeholders and vendors to refine criteria and methodologies.

9. Update and Reassess

Regular Updates

- Schedule regular updates to the materiality assessment process, considering changes in the business environment, regulatory landscape, and vendor ecosystem.

Reassessment Triggers

- Identify triggers for reassessment, such as significant changes in a vendor's financial health, new regulatory requirements, or internal organizational changes.

Implementation Example

Step 1: Define Objectives and Scope

- Objective: Identify high-risk vendors to prioritize risk management efforts.
- Scope: Assess all IT service providers, focusing on data sensitivity and operational dependence.

Step 2: Develop Assessment Criteria

- Criteria: Financial stability (25%), operational dependence (30%), data sensitivity (20%), compliance history (15%), reputational impact (10%).
- Weights: Financial stability (25%), operational dependence (30%), data sensitivity (20%), compliance history (15%), reputational impact (10%).

Step 3: Data Collection

- Internal: Gather contract details, performance reports, and incident logs.
- External: Obtain credit ratings, industry benchmarks, and news articles.
- Questionnaires: Send detailed questionnaires to IT service providers.

Step 4: Vendor Evaluation

- Calculate scores based on collected data and criteria.
- Analyze data using statistical tools and visualization methods.

Step 5: Risk Ranking and Prioritization

- Rank vendors based on scores.
- Prioritize the top 10% of vendors with highest materiality scores for immediate action.

Step 6: Reporting and Documentation

- Prepare a comprehensive report with findings and recommendations.
- Share report with senior management and risk management teams.

Step 7: Action Planning

- Develop mitigation plans for high-priority vendors, including enhanced monitoring and compliance checks.
- Allocate resources and responsibilities to manage these vendors.

Step 8: Continuous Monitoring and Review

- Implement real-time monitoring tools for high-priority vendors.
- Conduct quarterly reviews to update materiality scores and adjust priorities.

Step 9: Update and Reassess

- Schedule annual updates to the materiality assessment process.
- Trigger reassessment for significant vendor changes or new regulatory requirements.

By following this materiality assessment process, organizations can systematically evaluate and prioritize their vendors, ensuring that they focus their risk management efforts on the most critical relationships. This proactive approach enhances overall vendor management and helps mitigate potential risks effectively.

The impact of vendor scores on an organization can be profound, influencing various aspects of risk management, operational efficiency, strategic planning, and regulatory compliance. Vendor scores provide a quantifiable measure of the risks and performance associated with each vendor, allowing organizations to make informed decisions. Here's a comprehensive analysis of the impact of vendor scores:

1. Risk Management

Identification of High-Risk Vendors

- Vendor scores help identify vendors that pose significant risks due to factors such as financial instability, poor security practices, or non-compliance with regulations. High-risk vendors can be prioritized for more frequent audits, stricter monitoring, and comprehensive risk mitigation strategies.

Enhanced Risk Mitigation

- By quantifying risks, vendor scores enable organizations to implement targeted risk mitigation measures. For example, a vendor with a low data security score may require enhanced cybersecurity controls and regular vulnerability assessments.

Proactive Risk Management

- Continuous monitoring and updating of vendor scores allow organizations to proactively manage emerging risks. If a vendor's score deteriorates due to a significant event (e.g., a data breach), the organization can take immediate action to mitigate potential impacts.

2. Operational Efficiency

Resource Allocation

- Vendor scores help allocate resources more efficiently by focusing attention on critical vendors. For instance, vendors with high operational dependence and low performance scores may require additional support and resources to ensure seamless operations.

Performance Improvement

- By regularly evaluating vendor performance through scores, organizations can identify areas for improvement and work collaboratively with vendors to enhance service quality. This leads to better operational outcomes and improved vendor relationships.

Contract Management

- Vendor scores can inform contract negotiations and renewals. Vendors with high scores in areas like service quality and compliance can be rewarded with longer contracts or better terms, while those with low scores may face stricter terms or contract termination.

3. Strategic Planning

Vendor Selection and Diversification

- Vendor scores play a crucial role in the vendor selection process. Organizations can use these scores to choose vendors that align with their strategic goals and risk appetite. Additionally, scores can help in diversifying the vendor base to avoid over-reliance on a few high-risk vendors.

Strategic Partnerships

- High-scoring vendors can be identified as potential strategic partners. These vendors can be involved in long-term projects, collaborative innovations, and strategic initiatives that drive the organization's growth and competitiveness.

Supply Chain Resilience

- By assessing and scoring the risks associated with each vendor, organizations can build a more resilient supply chain. Understanding the risk profile of each vendor helps in developing contingency plans and ensuring continuity in case of disruptions.

4. Regulatory Compliance

Regulatory Adherence

- Vendor scores that include compliance metrics ensure that vendors adhere to relevant regulations and industry standards. This reduces the risk of regulatory breaches and associated penalties.

Audit and Reporting

- Vendor scores facilitate easier audit and reporting processes. Organizations can quickly identify vendors that may need closer scrutiny during audits based on their compliance scores.

Regulatory Changes

- Scores can be adjusted to reflect changes in regulatory requirements. This ensures that the organization's vendor risk management practices remain up-to-date and compliant with evolving regulations.

5. Financial Impact

Cost Management

- By identifying vendors that pose financial risks (e.g., those with poor financial stability scores), organizations can manage costs more effectively. This includes renegotiating payment terms or finding alternative suppliers to avoid potential financial losses.

Investment Decisions

- Vendor scores inform investment decisions, such as whether to invest in new technology or infrastructure provided by a vendor. High-scoring vendors are more likely to be considered for strategic investments.

Insurance and Risk Transfer

- Vendor scores can impact the organization's insurance policies and risk transfer strategies. Vendors with low risk scores may help in negotiating better insurance premiums or coverage terms.

6. Reputation Management

Maintaining Brand Integrity

- Vendors with high reputational risk scores can harm the organization's brand. By identifying and managing these vendors proactively, organizations can protect their reputation and maintain stakeholder trust.

Crisis Management

- In the event of a vendor-related crisis, vendor scores provide critical information for managing the situation. Organizations can prioritize their response based on the risk profile and impact of the affected vendor.

Implementation of Vendor Scores Impact

Step 1: Develop and Standardize Scoring Criteria

- Establish clear and standardized criteria for scoring vendors across various risk and performance categories. Ensure these criteria are aligned with the organization's risk management framework and strategic objectives.

Step 2: Integrate with Risk Management Processes

- Integrate vendor scoring into the organization's overall risk management processes. Use scores to inform risk assessments, audits, and monitoring activities.

Step 3: Continuous Monitoring and Review

- Implement continuous monitoring tools to track changes in vendor scores. Regularly review and update scores to reflect current data and emerging risks.

Step 4: Communicate and Collaborate with Vendors

- Share relevant score information with vendors to promote transparency and collaboration. Work with vendors to address areas of concern and improve their scores.

Step 5: Report and Utilize Scores for Decision Making

- Incorporate vendor scores into regular risk management reports and decision-making processes. Use these scores to prioritize actions, allocate resources, and guide strategic planning.

Conclusion

Vendor scores significantly impact an organization's ability to manage risks, enhance operational efficiency, ensure regulatory compliance, and make strategic decisions. By systematically assessing and monitoring vendor risks through a comprehensive scoring system, organizations can prioritize their efforts, protect their interests, and drive better outcomes in their vendor management practices.

Chapter 13: Vendor Selection Tips

Selecting the right vendors is crucial for maintaining a robust and efficient supply chain, ensuring quality service delivery, and minimizing risks. Here are detailed tips for vendor selection to help organizations make informed and strategic decisions:

1. Define Requirements and Objectives

Identify Needs

Clearly define what products or services you need from a vendor. Specify technical requirements, quality standards, and expected outcomes.

Set Objectives

Establish clear objectives for the vendor relationship, such as cost reduction, quality improvement, innovation, or risk mitigation.

Develop Detailed Specifications

Create comprehensive specifications for the products or services needed. Include performance criteria, compliance requirements, and delivery timelines.

2. Conduct Market Research

Identify Potential Vendors

Use various sources such as industry reports, trade associations, and online directories to identify potential vendors.

Evaluate Market Trends

Understand market trends, pricing structures, and emerging technologies to make informed decisions.

Check References and Reviews

Look for reviews, testimonials, and references from other clients to gauge the vendor's reputation and reliability.

3. Pre-Qualification and Shortlisting

Set Pre-Qualification Criteria

Establish criteria for pre-qualifying vendors, such as financial stability, industry experience, certifications, and regulatory compliance.

Create a Vendor Shortlist

Based on pre-qualification criteria, create a shortlist of vendors that meet your initial requirements.

4. Request for Proposal (RFP) or Request for Information (RFI)

Prepare RFP/RFI Documents

Develop comprehensive RFP or RFI documents detailing your requirements, evaluation criteria, and submission guidelines.

Distribute RFP/RFI

Send the RFP/RFI to shortlisted vendors and provide a timeline for submission.

Evaluate Responses

Assess the responses based on predefined criteria, such as technical capabilities, pricing, service levels, and compliance.

5. Assess Vendor Capabilities

Technical Competence

Evaluate the vendor's technical capabilities and expertise. Ensure they have the necessary skills, technology, and infrastructure to meet your requirements.

Financial Stability

Assess the vendor's financial health by reviewing financial statements, credit ratings, and financial ratios.

Operational Capacity

Check the vendor's production capacity, scalability, and ability to handle large or complex orders.

6. Evaluate Risk Factors

Risk Assessment

Conduct a thorough risk assessment covering financial, operational, compliance, and reputational risks.

Vendor Risk Mitigation

Evaluate the vendor's risk mitigation strategies, including business continuity plans, disaster recovery processes, and security measures.

Compliance and Regulatory Risks

Ensure the vendor complies with all relevant laws, regulations, and industry standards.

7. Assess Quality and Performance

Quality Management Systems

Evaluate the vendor's quality management systems, such as ISO certifications and adherence to quality standards.

Performance Metrics

Review the vendor's performance metrics, including delivery times, defect rates, and customer satisfaction scores.

Site Visits and Audits

Conduct site visits and audits to assess the vendor's facilities, processes, and adherence to quality standards.

8. Consider Cost and Value

Cost Analysis

Perform a detailed cost analysis, including unit prices, total cost of ownership, and hidden costs.

Value Proposition

Consider the overall value proposition, including the vendor's ability to deliver innovative solutions, improve efficiency, and support strategic goals.

Negotiate Terms

Negotiate favorable terms and conditions, including pricing, payment terms, delivery schedules, and service levels.

9. Evaluate Cultural Fit and Communication

Cultural Alignment

Assess the cultural fit between your organization and the vendor. Ensure that the vendor's values, ethics, and working styles align with yours.

Communication and Collaboration

Evaluate the vendor's communication practices, responsiveness, and willingness to collaborate. Effective communication is essential for a successful partnership.

Relationship Management

Consider the vendor's approach to relationship management, including their commitment to building long-term partnerships and addressing issues proactively.

10. Pilot Testing and Trials

Conduct Pilot Tests

Before committing to a long-term contract, conduct pilot tests or trials to evaluate the vendor's capabilities in a real-world scenario.

Monitor Performance

Monitor the vendor's performance during the pilot phase and gather feedback from relevant stakeholders.

Evaluate Results

Assess the results of the pilot tests and determine if the vendor meets your expectations and requirements.

11. Formalize the Contract

Draft Detailed Contracts

Draft detailed contracts that clearly outline the terms and conditions, including scope of work, pricing, delivery schedules, performance metrics, and penalties for non-compliance.

Include SLAs

Include Service Level Agreements (SLAs) to define performance standards and expectations. SLAs should cover areas such as response times, uptime guarantees, and quality standards. Always create two sets – one for the BAU and the other for BCM.

Review Legal and Compliance Issues

Ensure that the contract complies with all relevant laws and regulations. Seek legal advice to address any potential issues or ambiguities.

12. Establish Governance and Monitoring

Define Governance Structure

Establish a governance structure to manage the vendor relationship, including roles, responsibilities, and escalation procedures.

Implement Monitoring Tools

Use monitoring tools and performance dashboards to track the vendor's performance against agreed-upon metrics and SLAs.

Regular Reviews

Conduct regular performance reviews and feedback sessions with the vendor to address any issues and continuously improve the relationship.

13. Plan for Contingencies and Exit

Contingency Planning

Develop contingency plans to address potential disruptions, such as vendor insolvency, supply chain disruptions, or quality issues.

Exit Strategy

Define an exit strategy in the contract to ensure a smooth transition if the vendor relationship needs to be terminated. Include terms for data transfer, knowledge sharing, and continuity of services.

14. Foster Continuous Improvement

Encourage Innovation

Encourage vendors to propose innovative solutions and improvements. Foster a collaborative environment where both parties can benefit from shared knowledge and expertise.

Performance Improvement Plans

Work with vendors to develop performance improvement plans if they fall short of expectations. Provide support and resources to help them meet your standards.

Regular Training and Development

Invest in regular training and development for both your team and the vendor's team to enhance skills, knowledge, and collaboration.

By following these comprehensive vendor selection tips, organizations can build strong, reliable, and strategic vendor relationships that drive business success and mitigate risks.

Chapter 14: The Role of AI in Third Party Risk Management

No book today can be complete without discussing AI; hence I am devoting a chapter to this content.

Introduction

In today's complex and interconnected global business environment, managing third-party risks has become a critical aspect of ensuring organizational resilience and compliance. Artificial Intelligence (AI) will be increasingly leveraged to enhance the efficiency and effectiveness of Third Party Risk Management (TPRM). This chapter explores how AI technologies can/ will transform TPRM processes, enabling organizations to better identify, assess, mitigate, and monitor risks associated with their third-party relationships.

The Importance of AI in TPRM

AI offers several advantages in TPRM, including the ability to process large volumes of data, identify patterns, predict risks, and automate routine tasks (so the Chief Vendor Data Manager will be very happy). These capabilities allow organizations to:

- Improve risk identification and assessment.
- Enhance decision-making with data-driven insights.
- Increase efficiency through automation.
- Strengthen continuous monitoring and compliance efforts.

AI Applications in TPRM

1. Risk Identification and Assessment

AI algorithms can analyze vast amounts of structured and unstructured data to identify potential risks associated with third parties. Key applications include:

- **Data Mining and Analysis**: AI-powered tools can mine data from various sources, such as news articles, social media, financial reports, and regulatory filings, to detect early warning signals for emerging risks.
- **Natural Language Processing (NLP)**: NLP can be used to analyze textual data and extract relevant information about third-party entities, such as legal issues, financial instability, or negative public sentiment.
- **Predictive Analytics**: AI models can predict the likelihood of future risks by analyzing historical data and identifying patterns that precede risk events.

2. Due Diligence and Onboarding

AI can streamline the due diligence and onboarding process by automating tasks and providing deeper insights into third-party entities:

- **Automated Screening**: AI-powered screening tools can quickly process large volumes of data to identify red flags, such as sanctions, adverse media coverage, or previous legal violations.
- **Enhanced Background Checks**: AI can aggregate and analyze data from multiple sources to provide a comprehensive view of a third party's background, including their financial health, legal history, and reputation.
- **Risk Scoring**: AI models can assign risk scores to third parties based on various factors, enabling organizations to prioritize their due diligence efforts and focus on high-risk entities.

3. Contract Management and Compliance

AI can enhance contract management and compliance monitoring by automating processes and providing real-time insights:

- **Contract Analysis**: AI tools can analyze contract language to identify potential risks, such as unfavorable terms, compliance gaps, or clauses that could lead to disputes.
- **Regulatory Compliance**: AI can continuously monitor regulatory changes and assess their impact on third-party relationships, ensuring ongoing compliance with relevant laws and standards.
- **Automated Alerts**: AI-driven systems can generate real-time alerts for compliance violations or changes in a third party's risk profile, allowing for timely intervention.

4. Continuous Monitoring and Risk Mitigation

AI can enable continuous monitoring of third-party risks, providing organizations with the ability to proactively mitigate potential issues:

- **Real-Time Data Integration**: AI systems can integrate data from multiple sources in real time, providing a holistic view of third-party risks and enabling timely decision-making.
- **Anomaly Detection**: AI can identify unusual patterns or behaviors that may indicate emerging risks, such as changes in transaction patterns, deviations from expected performance, or signs of financial distress.
- **Scenario Analysis**: AI-powered scenario analysis can simulate various risk scenarios and their potential impact, helping organizations to develop effective risk mitigation strategies.

5. Fraud Detection and Prevention

AI can be instrumental in detecting and preventing fraud within third-party relationships:

- **Behavioral Analysis**: AI can analyze behavioral patterns to identify anomalies that may indicate fraudulent activities, such as unusual spending patterns or suspicious transaction behaviors.
- **Machine Learning Models**: These models can learn from historical fraud cases to improve their ability to detect new and evolving fraud tactics, reducing false positives and improving detection accuracy.
- **Fraud Risk Scoring**: AI can assign fraud risk scores to third parties based on various indicators, allowing organizations to focus their fraud prevention efforts on high-risk entities.

Case Studies

Again, I do not have any proof, but the following examples are based on easily available information on the internet.

Example 1: IBM's Watson for TPRM

IBM's Watson, an AI-powered cognitive computing system, is being used to enhance TPRM processes. Watson can analyze vast amounts of unstructured data to identify potential risks and provide actionable insights. For example, Watson can process news articles, social media posts, and regulatory filings to detect early warning signs of risk, such as financial instability or legal issues. By leveraging Watson's capabilities, organizations can improve their risk identification and assessment processes, making more informed decisions about their third-party relationships. [ii]

Example 2: Deloitte's AI-Driven TPRM Solutions

Deloitte uses AI-driven solutions to enhance its TPRM services. These solutions include AI-powered tools for automated screening, risk scoring, and continuous monitoring. Deloitte's AI tools can quickly process large volumes of data to identify red flags, such as sanctions or adverse media coverage. By using AI to streamline due diligence and onboarding processes, Deloitte helps its clients improve the efficiency and effectiveness of their TPRM efforts. [iii]

Future Trends in AI and TPRM

1. Enhanced Predictive Capabilities

As AI technology continues to evolve, its predictive capabilities will become more advanced. Future AI models will be able to predict risks with greater accuracy, enabling organizations to take proactive measures to mitigate potential issues before they materialize.

2. Integration with Blockchain Technology

The integration of AI with blockchain technology will provide even greater transparency and traceability in third-party relationships. Blockchain can securely record transactions and other interactions, while AI can analyze this data to identify risks and ensure compliance with regulatory requirements.

3. Increased Use of Robotic Process Automation (RPA)

RPA combined with AI will further automate routine TPRM tasks, such as data entry, document processing, and compliance checks. This will free up resources for more strategic activities, such as risk analysis and mitigation.

4. Enhanced Focus on Cybersecurity Risks

As cybersecurity threats continue to evolve, AI will play a crucial role in identifying and mitigating these risks in third-party relationships. AI-powered tools will be able to detect and respond to cyber threats in real time, helping organizations protect their sensitive data and maintain the integrity of their supply chains.

5. Greater Adoption of AI in Small and Medium-Sized Enterprises (SMEs)

As AI technology becomes more accessible and affordable, SMEs will increasingly adopt AI-powered TPRM solutions. This will enable smaller organizations to benefit from the same advanced risk management capabilities as larger enterprises, leveling the playing field in the global market.

Conclusion

Artificial Intelligence is revolutionizing Third Party Risk Management by providing powerful tools for risk identification, assessment, mitigation, and monitoring. By leveraging AI technologies, organizations can enhance their TPRM processes, improve decision-making, and ensure compliance with regulatory requirements. As AI continues to evolve, its role in TPRM will become even more critical, helping organizations navigate the complexities of managing third-party risks in an increasingly interconnected world. This chapter highlights the transformative potential of AI in TPRM and serves as a call to action for organizations to embrace AI-driven solutions to enhance their risk management strategies.

The Last Chapter: Responsible Sourcing

I could not have closed the book without writing this chapter. This would be linked to reality – the ESG, Sustainability, Resilience, and Business Continuity all are related to this.

Introduction

Responsible sourcing refers to the procurement of goods and services in a manner that considers ethical, environmental, and social factors. In the context of Third Party Risk Management (TPRM), responsible sourcing is crucial for ensuring that an organization's supply chain is resilient, ethical, and compliant with various standards and regulations. It goes beyond traditional procurement practices by incorporating sustainability and responsibility into the decision-making process, thereby reducing risks associated with third-party relationships.

The Business Case for Responsible Sourcing

Benefits of Responsible Sourcing

Responsible sourcing offers numerous benefits, including:

- **Risk Mitigation**: By selecting suppliers who adhere to ethical standards, organizations can reduce risks related to fraud, corruption, and non-compliance.
- **Reputation Management**: Companies that prioritize responsible sourcing enhance their brand reputation and build trust with stakeholders.
- **Compliance**: Adhering to responsible sourcing practices helps organizations comply with regulations and avoid legal penalties.

Impact on Supply Chain Resilience

A resilient supply chain is one that can adapt to disruptions and continue operations smoothly. Responsible sourcing contributes to supply chain resilience by:

- Ensuring suppliers follow sustainable practices, which reduces the risk of supply chain disruptions due to environmental or social issues.
- Promoting transparency and traceability, allowing organizations to quickly identify and address potential risks.

Key Principles of Responsible Sourcing

Ethical Sourcing

Ethical sourcing involves procuring goods and services in a manner that respects human rights and labor standards. Key elements include:

- Ensuring fair wages and safe working conditions for workers.
- Prohibiting child labor and forced labor.
- Promoting diversity, equity, and inclusion in the supply chain. I draw attention to my detailed blog at https://www.damandevsood.com/post/beyond-gender-and-ethnicity-embracing-true-diversity-and-inclusion-and-equity-in-the-workplace .

Environmental Sustainability

Environmental sustainability focuses on reducing the ecological footprint of the supply chain. This includes:

- Sourcing materials from sustainable sources.

- Minimizing waste and emissions during production and transportation.
- Encouraging suppliers to adopt eco-friendly practices.
- Following the principles of Total Cost of Ownership and Lifecycle Assessment

A word of caution here is to avoid SustainabilityWashing. I draw attention to my detailed blogs at https://www.damandevsood.com/post/what-is-a-real-sustainable-company and https://www.damandevsood.com/post/what-is-a-real-sustainable-company-part-ii .

Social Responsibility

Social responsibility entails contributing to the well-being of communities and society at large. This can be achieved by:

- Supporting local communities through fair trade practices.
- Investing in social programs that benefit supplier communities.
- Ensuring that supplier practices align with the organization's values and social commitments.

AML, Anti-Bribery, and Anti-Corruption

Incorporating anti money laundering, anti-bribery, and anti-corruption measures into responsible sourcing ensures that:

- Screening for involvement in money laundering activities.
- Monitoring transactions to detect and prevent money laundering.
- Enforcing Anti-bribery policies to prevent unethical practices.
- Adherence to anti-corruption laws and regulations, ensuring fair business practices.

I will strongly recommend these to be done at both ends – the customers as well as the third parties.

Insider Risk Management

Insider risk management involves identifying and mitigating risks posed by individuals within the organization or its supply chain who may have access to sensitive information or critical systems. This includes:

- Implementing robust access controls and monitoring systems to detect unusual activities.
- Conducting background checks on employees, contractors, and suppliers to ensure they meet ethical and security standards.
- Establishing clear policies and procedures for reporting and addressing insider threats.

I draw attention to my detailed blog at https://www.damandevsood.com/post/leadership-trust-and-risk-management-safeguarding-organizations-from-insider-threats .

Implementing Responsible Sourcing

Establishing Standards and Policies

To implement responsible sourcing, organizations should establish clear standards and policies. These should outline:

- Ethical, environmental, and social criteria for supplier selection.
- Requirements for supplier conduct and performance.
- Procedures for monitoring and enforcing compliance.

Supplier Evaluation and Selection

Evaluating and selecting suppliers based on responsible sourcing criteria involves:

- Conducting thorough due diligence to assess potential suppliers' adherence to standards, including AML, anti-bribery, anti-corruption, and insider risk management policies.
- Using tools such as supplier scorecards and audits to evaluate performance.
- Selecting suppliers who demonstrate a commitment to responsible practices.

Continuous Monitoring and Improvement

Responsible sourcing is an ongoing process that requires continuous monitoring and improvement. Organizations should:

- Regularly audit suppliers to ensure compliance with responsible sourcing standards.
- Provide training and support to help suppliers improve their practices.
- Encourage feedback and collaboration to identify areas for improvement.

Challenges and Solutions

Common Challenges in Responsible Sourcing

Implementing responsible sourcing can be challenging due to factors such as:

- **Complex Supply Chains**: Managing responsible sourcing across complex, global supply chains can be difficult.
- **Lack of Transparency**: Limited visibility into suppliers' practices can hinder efforts to ensure compliance.
- **Cost Considerations**: Responsible sourcing may involve higher costs, which can be a barrier for some organizations.

Strategies to Overcome These Challenges

To overcome these challenges, organizations can:

- **Leverage Technology**: Use technology such as blockchain for supply chain transparency and traceability.
- **Collaborate with Stakeholders**: Work with industry groups, NGOs, and other stakeholders to promote responsible sourcing.
- **Invest in Training and Capacity Building**: Support suppliers in improving their practices through training and capacity-building initiatives.

Examples

I have no proof of these, am writing this based on information available on the internet.

Example 1: Apple Inc.'s Ethical Sourcing Program

Apple Inc. has made significant strides in ethical sourcing. The company conducts rigorous supplier audits to ensure compliance with its Supplier Code of Conduct, which includes standards for labor practices, health and safety, and environmental protection. Apple has been able to significantly reduce instances of labor violations, such as excessive working hours and underpayment, in its supply chain. In addition, Apple has committed to sourcing minerals in a responsible way, ensuring that they do not fund conflict or involve human rights abuses. A case study may be looked at https://europeanpartnership-responsibleminerals.eu/blog/view/ccae57d3-e04b-4b53-8169-3898831666ac/case-study-apple .

This should be read with a pinch of salt, as Apple at the same time is also accused of on purpose reducing the life of its products programmatically.

Example 2: Unilever's Environmental Initiatives

Unilever, a leading manufacturer of consumer goods, has been at the forefront of environmental sustainability. The company's Sustainable Living Plan aims to decouple its growth from its environmental footprint while increasing its positive social impact. Unilever sources materials from certified sustainable sources and has committed to reducing its greenhouse gas emissions, water use, and waste production. These efforts have not only reduced the company's environmental impact but also enhanced its reputation as an industry leader in sustainability.[iv]

Example 3: Starbucks' Social Responsibility Efforts

Starbucks has a comprehensive approach to social responsibility, particularly through its Coffee and Farmer Equity (C.A.F.E.) Practices. This program sets standards for product quality, economic accountability, social responsibility, and environmental leadership. By investing in fair trade practices and social programs, Starbucks has helped improve the livelihoods of coffee farmers and their communities around the world. The company provides training and support to farmers to promote sustainable farming practices and improve their productivity and income.[v]

Example 4: HSBC's AML and Anti-Corruption Measures

HSBC, one of the world's largest banking and financial services organizations, has implemented stringent AML and anti-corruption measures to ensure compliance with global regulations. The bank uses advanced monitoring systems to detect and prevent money laundering and financial crimes. HSBC conducts thorough due diligence on its clients and suppliers to mitigate the risk of financial crimes. These measures have helped HSBC maintain high ethical standards and reduce the risk of regulatory penalties.

At the same time, HSBC has been fined for failing in its AML practices - https://www.fca.org.uk/news/press-releases/fca-fines-hsbc-bank-plc-deficient-transaction-monitoring-controls - this establishes the importance of the role and powers of the Regulators.

Example 5: Google's Insider Risk Management Program

Google has developed a comprehensive insider risk management program that includes robust access controls, continuous monitoring, and regular background checks on employees and contractors. The company uses advanced analytics and machine learning to detect unusual behavior that could indicate potential insider threats. Google's approach includes clear policies for reporting and addressing insider threats, which helps to protect its intellectual property and maintain the integrity and security of its operations.

Future Trends in Responsible Sourcing

Technological Advancements

Advancements in technology, such as artificial intelligence and blockchain, are transforming responsible sourcing by providing greater visibility and traceability in supply chains. These technologies enable organizations to monitor supplier practices more effectively and ensure compliance with responsible sourcing standards.

Evolving Regulatory Landscape

As regulations around ethical and sustainable practices continue to evolve (I have devoted one full chapter on this concept earlier in the book), organizations will need to stay abreast of changes and adapt their sourcing strategies accordingly. This includes complying with new laws and standards related to environmental protection, human rights, anti-money laundering, anti-bribery, insider risk management, corporate social responsibility, corporate governance, and DEI etc.

Increasing Consumer Awareness

Consumers are becoming more aware of the ethical and environmental impact of their purchases. This growing awareness is driving demand for responsibly sourced products and putting pressure on companies to adopt responsible sourcing practices.

Conclusion

Responsible sourcing plays a critical role in Third Party Risk Management by ensuring that an organization's supply chain is ethical, sustainable, and resilient. By prioritizing responsible sourcing, companies can mitigate risks, enhance their reputation, and contribute to positive social and environmental outcomes. The integration of AML, anti-bribery, anti-corruption, and insider risk management measures is essential to maintaining high ethical standards and legal compliance. As the landscape of responsible sourcing continues to evolve, organizations must remain committed to continuous improvement and collaboration with stakeholders. This closing chapter serves as a call to action for companies to embrace responsible sourcing and integrate it into their overall TPRM.

One More Chapter: Technology Failures – Manual Workarounds

I was done with writing this book (only editing left) when this Crowdstrike incident (crisis?) happened.

There are differing views, I call it a Cyber Incident (not necessarily attack), caused by or induced by a third party failure (without failing itself). So, at the last moment it had to find a place in my book.

For long, a strategy for technology/ IT failure has been said to 'move to manual workarounds'. I sat to investigate whether we could really adopt manual workarounds! 10 key processes from 10 different industry sectors were investigated and found a place in the book as the 'One More Chapter: Technology Failures - Manual Workarounds' including these cases. And surprisingly this turned out to be the longest chapter in the book!

1. **Patient Record Management in Healthcare: The Feasibility of Manual Operations During Technology Failures**

Introduction

In modern healthcare, patient record management relies heavily on Electronic Health Record (EHR) systems. These systems facilitate the digital entry, storage, and retrieval of patient information, ensuring seamless sharing between healthcare providers. However, the dependency on technology raises the question: what happens when these systems fail? This article explores the current process of EHR-based patient record management, the feasibility of reverting to manual operations during technological outages, and the challenges and risks associated with such a transition.

Current Process and Dependencies

The assumption underlying this analysis is that patient records are fully managed using EHR systems. This digital process includes the entry, storage, and retrieval of patient information, with seamless sharing between healthcare providers. The efficiency of EHR systems relies on various technologies, including hardware (computers, servers), software (EHR systems), and third-party services (cloud storage, cybersecurity services). Additionally, skilled IT personnel are necessary to maintain and troubleshoot these systems.

Steps for Manual Operation

In the event of a technology failure, healthcare providers might consider transitioning to manual operations. The steps for manual patient record management would involve:

1. **Recording Patient Information on Paper**: Collecting patient details, medical history, and treatment information using physical forms.

2. **Storing Physical Records in Secure Locations**: Organizing and storing paper records in filing cabinets, ensuring they are secure and accessible only to authorized personnel.

3. **Accessing and Updating Patient Records Manually**: Manually retrieving records for updates and ensuring proper filing after each use.

Challenges and Risks of Manual Operations

Despite the feasibility of manual operations, several challenges and risks emerge:

- **Lack of Historical Patient Data**: Without access to the digital system, historical patient data will not be readily available. Fetching historical records from storage facilities may not be practical in emergency situations. Irony is that even the paper records are stored/ controlled/ accessed through IT/ Technology and hence appear to be unavailable!

- **Blank Forms Availability**: Manual processes require specific forms that may not be readily available. These forms should ideally be OCR-compatible to facilitate later digitization, adding complexity and cost to the business continuity solution.

- **Human Error**: Increased risk of inaccuracies in data entry and retrieval due to manual handling.

- **Time-Consuming**: Significantly more time required for recording, accessing, and updating patient information compared to automated systems.

- **Storage and Security**: Need for substantial physical storage space and challenges in maintaining the security and confidentiality of sensitive patient information.

- **Data Sharing**: Difficulty in sharing records between different healthcare providers, potentially leading to delays in patient care.

- **Reintegration into Digital Systems**: The necessity to digitize all manually recorded information once the technology is restored, which can be labor-intensive and prone to errors.

Feasibility Analysis

While manual record management is feasible, it is highly inefficient and filled with risks. The primary concerns include the risk of human error, time consumption, storage and security issues, difficulties in data sharing, and the burden of reintegrating data into digital systems. Additionally, the lack of access to historical patient data and the availability of appropriate blank forms are major barriers.

Recommendations

Given the constraints of manual operations, it may be more practical for healthcare providers to focus on minimizing downtime through robust IT disaster recovery plans and ensuring quick restoration of EHR systems. However, as seen in incidents like the CrowdStrike case, both primary and secondary systems can become inaccessible. Some critical patient information should be regularly backed up and stored in an easily accessible format that can be used during outages. This seems to suggest a return to paper records. Training staff on emergency protocols and temporary measures to manage patient care without full access to records is also essential. If a doctor or nurse makes a mistake in the absence of historical information, it could be fatal for the patient. Will patients and their caretakers be patient enough in such situations?

Ethical and Legal Considerations

In considering the feasibility of manual operations, ethical and legal questions arise. Can a hospital ethically or legally stop work until technology is restored? Can they refuse to treat critical patients or a pregnant woman about to deliver a baby due to technological failures? These questions highlight the importance of robust contingency plans that ensure continuity of patient care even during technology outages. While we must admit that business continuity or resilience doesn't make one failproof or foolproof, it is essential to mitigate the impact as much as possible.

Conclusion

This discussion remains inconclusive. The transition from paper to digital systems was driven by the need for efficiency and accuracy in patient record management. However, when technology fails, the records themselves remain intact, but access is disrupted, making backups ineffective. Resorting to paper records is impractical unless they are created simultaneously with digital entries, which is unreasonable.

Therefore, it is essential to set realistic expectations not only for healthcare providers but also for healthcare seekers and beneficiaries. While resilient IT systems can significantly reduce downtime, it cannot be entirely avoided. Both providers and patients must understand that certain situations will necessitate living with temporary downtimes. Although this may create discomfort, and in some cases critical issues, it is not underestimated. The focus should be on minimizing these periods through robust IT disaster recovery plans and ensuring that staff are prepared to manage patient care effectively during these outages. Setting appropriate expectations is key to navigating these challenges without making bold claims about the infallibility of IT systems.

2. Pharmaceutical: Logistics (a Supply Chain Management) Process During Technology Failures

Introduction

In the pharmaceutical industry, supply chain management is crucial for ensuring the timely delivery of medications and other essential products. The process heavily relies on sophisticated technology systems for tracking, inventory management, and logistics. This article explores the current process of technology-based supply chain management, the feasibility of reverting to manual operations during technological outages, and the challenges and risks associated with such a transition.

Current Process and Dependencies

The assumption underlying this analysis is that supply chain management in the pharmaceutical industry is fully managed using advanced software systems. These systems handle everything from order processing and inventory tracking to logistics and distribution. The efficiency of these systems relies on various technologies, including hardware (servers, computers), software (supply chain management systems), and third-party services (cloud services, cybersecurity). Additionally, skilled IT personnel are necessary to maintain and troubleshoot these systems.

Steps for Manual Operation

In the event of a technology failure, pharmaceutical companies might consider transitioning to manual operations. The steps for manual supply chain management would involve:

1. **Order Processing on Paper**: Collecting orders using physical forms and manual entry.

2. **Inventory Tracking Manually**: Using paper logs to track inventory levels and movements.

3. **Logistics Coordination via Phone and Paper**: Coordinating deliveries and shipments using phone calls and written records.

Challenges and Risks of Manual Operations

Despite the feasibility of manual operations, several challenges and risks emerge:

- **Is it One-Way-Down or Two-Ways:** You may be willing to receive orders and serve orders manually, but the other party (vendor or customer) may be up and running. So, it may be a challenge. This is how this process is different from Patient Health Records where technology was only at one end (healthcare provider) and poses more challenges immediately.

- **Lack of Real-Time Data**: Without access to digital systems, real-time tracking of inventory and shipments is impossible, leading to potential stockouts or overstock situations.

- **Human Error**: Increased risk of inaccuracies in data entry and tracking due to manual handling.

- **Time-Consuming**: Significantly more time required for processing orders, tracking inventory, and coordinating logistics compared to automated systems. Imagine manual loading and uploading of the supplies too.

- **Storage and Security**: Need for substantial physical storage space for paper records and challenges in maintaining the security of sensitive information. Once again, more complexity may be seen here – it's not just invoices, orders etc. that will pose a risk of storage, even the storage of raw material and finished goods will be a bigger challenge.

- **Data Sharing**: Difficulty in sharing information between different departments and partners, potentially leading to delays and miscommunication.

- **Reintegration into Digital Systems**: The necessity to digitize all manually recorded information once the technology is restored, which can be labor-intensive and prone to errors.

Feasibility Analysis

While manual supply chain management is feasible, it is highly inefficient and filled with risks. The primary concerns include the risk of human error, time consumption, storage and security issues, difficulties in data sharing, and the burden of reintegrating data into digital systems.

Recommendations

Given the constraints of manual operations, it may be more practical for pharmaceutical companies to focus on minimizing downtime through robust IT disaster recovery plans and ensuring quick restoration of supply chain management systems. Critical supply chain information should be regularly backed up and stored in an easily accessible format that can be used during outages. Training staff on emergency protocols and temporary measures to manage supply chain operations without full access to records is also essential.

The admittance here is that an event of the type of Crowdstrike can bring both the primary and the secondary down at the same time. Better said – an event of this type can make both primary and secondary inaccessible at the same time.

Ethical and Legal Considerations

In considering the feasibility of manual operations, ethical and legal questions arise. Can a pharmaceutical company ethically or legally stop operations until technology is restored? What are the implications for patients waiting for essential medications? These questions highlight the importance of robust contingency plans that ensure continuity of supply chain operations even during technology outages.

Conclusion

This discussion remains inconclusive. The transition from paper to digital systems was driven by the need for efficiency and accuracy in supply chain management. However, when technology fails, access to records is disrupted, making backups ineffective. Resorting to paper records is impractical unless they are created simultaneously with digital entries, which is unreasonable.

Therefore, it is essential to set realistic expectations not only for pharmaceutical companies but also for their partners and beneficiaries. While resilient IT systems can significantly reduce downtime, it cannot be entirely avoided. Both providers and beneficiaries must understand that certain situations will necessitate living with temporary downtimes. The focus should be on minimizing these periods through robust IT disaster recovery plans and ensuring that staff are prepared to manage supply chain operations effectively during these outages. Setting appropriate expectations is key to navigating these challenges without making bold claims about the infallibility of IT systems.

Another admittance here is that a logistics/ supply chain management down time in a pharma company may not have (or may have less) life threatening situation as compared to the patient health records in a healthcare provider's IT failure.

3. Utilities: Power Grid Management Process During Technology Failures

Introduction

The management of power grids in the utilities sector is heavily reliant on advanced technology systems. These systems facilitate the monitoring, control, and distribution of electricity across regions. This article explores the current process of technology-based power grid management, the feasibility of reverting to manual operations during technological outages, and the challenges and risks associated with such a transition.

Current Process and Dependencies

The assumption underlying this analysis is that power grid management is fully managed using advanced technology systems. These systems handle everything from real-time monitoring and load balancing to fault detection and outage management. The efficiency of these systems relies on various technologies, including hardware (servers, sensors), software (SCADA systems), and third-party services (cloud services, cybersecurity). Additionally, skilled IT and engineering personnel are necessary to maintain and troubleshoot these systems. At first look it may appear that power grid management process won't need access to historical data but other sub-processes do need it e.g. Grid Planning and Design, Operational Efficiency, Fault Detection and Analysis, Demand Response, Emergency Response and Recovery, Regulatory Compliance and Reporting etc.

Steps for Manual Operation

In the event of a technology failure, utility companies might consider transitioning to manual operations. The steps for manual power grid management would involve:

1. **Monitoring Grid Conditions Manually**: Using physical gauges and instruments to monitor grid conditions.

2. **Manual Load Balancing**: Coordinating load distribution using phone calls and written logs.

3. **Fault Detection and Outage Management**: Identifying and responding to faults and outages through manual inspections and coordination.

4. **Maintain Records/ readings Manually**: Record various parameters on paper forms.

All above have extremely low feasibility.

Challenges and Risks of Manual Operations

Despite the feasibility of manual operations, several challenges and risks emerge:

- **Lack of Real-Time Data**: Without access to digital systems, real-time monitoring and control of the power grid is impossible, leading to potential imbalances and outages.

- **Human Error**: Increased risk of inaccuracies in monitoring and control due to manual handling.

- **Time-Consuming**: Significantly more time required for monitoring, load balancing, and outage management compared to automated systems.

- **Tools**: Availability and calibration of manual tools as well as their maintenance mad usage will be great challenges.

- **Coordination Challenges**: Difficulty in coordinating actions between different teams and locations, potentially leading to delays in response.

- **Data Sharing**: Difficulty in sharing information between different departments and partners, potentially leading to miscommunication and inefficiencies.

- **Manual Recording**: Not only the forms/ OCR forms may be absent, even their usage and storage will be added ones.

- **Reintegration into Digital Systems**: The necessity to digitize all manually recorded information once the technology is restored, which can be labor-intensive and prone to errors.

Feasibility Analysis

While manual power grid management is feasible, it is highly inefficient and filled with risks. The primary concerns include the risk of human error, time consumption, coordination challenges, calibration-usage-and-maintenance of manual tools, and the burden of reintegrating data into digital systems.

Recommendations

Given the constraints of manual operations, it may be more practical for utility companies to focus on minimizing downtime through robust IT disaster recovery plans and ensuring quick restoration of power grid management systems. Critical grid management information should be regularly backed up and stored in an easily accessible format that can be used during outages. Training staff on emergency protocols and temporary measures to manage grid operations without full access to records is also essential.

Ethical and Legal Considerations

In considering the feasibility of manual operations, ethical and legal questions arise. Can a utility company ethically or legally stop operations until technology is restored? What are the implications for customers relying on continuous power supply? These questions highlight the importance of robust contingency plans that ensure continuity of grid operations even during technology outages. So, this appears to be an important process and see the cascading effect – power grid fails due to technology failure, that results into failure of all technology in all industries and all processes! I dare some company to test such a scenario even as a tabletop exercise – I will be happy to design, develop, and deliver!

Conclusion

This discussion remains inconclusive. The transition from manual/ paper to digital systems was driven by the need for efficiency and accuracy in power grid management. However, when technology fails, access to records is disrupted, making backups ineffective. Resorting to manual operations and paper records is impractical unless they are created simultaneously with digital entries, which is unreasonable.

Therefore, it is essential to set realistic expectations not only for utility companies but also for their customers and stakeholders. While resilient IT systems can significantly reduce downtime, it cannot be entirely avoided. Both providers and beneficiaries must understand that certain situations will necessitate living with temporary downtimes. The focus should be on minimizing these periods through robust IT disaster recovery plans and ensuring that staff are prepared to manage grid operations effectively during these outages. Setting appropriate expectations is key to navigating these challenges without making bold claims about the infallibility of IT systems.

4. Telecom: Network Operations Process During Technology Failures

Introduction

In the telecommunications industry, network operations rely heavily on advanced technology systems. These systems facilitate the monitoring, control, and maintenance of telecom networks to ensure uninterrupted service. This article explores the current process of technology-based network operations, the feasibility of reverting to manual operations and manual record keeping during technological outages, and the challenges and risks associated with such a transition.

Current Process and Dependencies

The assumption underlying this analysis is that telecom network operations are fully managed using advanced technology systems. These systems handle everything from real-time monitoring and fault detection to network configuration and optimization. At the broadest level even billing and invoicing may be considered as part of Network Operations and are all fully automated. The efficiency of these systems relies on various technologies, including hardware (servers, network equipment), software (network management systems), and third-party services (cloud services, cybersecurity). Additionally, skilled IT and network personnel are necessary to maintain and troubleshoot these systems.

Steps for Manual Operation

In the event of a technology failure, telecom companies might consider transitioning to manual operations. The steps for manual network operations would involve:

1. **Monitoring Network Conditions Manually**: Using physical instruments and tools to monitor network conditions.

2. **Manual Fault Detection and Repair**: Identifying and repairing network issues through manual inspections and coordination.

3. **Network Configuration and Optimization**: Adjusting network settings and optimizing performance manually using written records and physical controls.

Challenges and Risks of Manual Operations

Despite the feasibility of manual operations, several challenges and risks emerge:

- **Lack of Real-Time Data**: Without access to digital systems, real-time monitoring and control of the network is impossible, leading to potential service disruptions.

- **Human Error**: Increased risk of inaccuracies in monitoring, fault detection, and network configuration due to manual handling.

- **Time-Consuming**: Significantly more time required for monitoring, fault detection, and network optimization compared to automated systems.

- **Coordination Challenges**: Difficulty in coordinating actions between different teams and locations, potentially leading to delays in response.

- **Data Sharing**: Difficulty in sharing information between different departments and partners, potentially leading to miscommunication and inefficiencies.

- **Reintegration into Digital Systems**: The necessity to digitize all manually recorded information once the technology is restored, which can be labor-intensive and prone to errors.

Feasibility Analysis

While manual network operations are feasible, they are highly inefficient and filled with risks. The primary concerns include the risk of human error, time consumption, coordination challenges, and the burden of reintegrating data into digital systems.

The feasibility of moving to manual operations seems to be very low for this process. Here is how telecom networks are different (and hence manual operations more challenging-less feasible) compared to power networks –

power networks are all physical – either over or under the ground, while telecom networks are wired as well as wireless and under the ground, over the ground, in the air and under the water also!

Recommendations

Given the constraints of manual operations, it may be more practical for telecom companies to focus on minimizing downtime through robust IT disaster recovery plans and ensuring quick restoration of network management systems. Critical network management information should be regularly backed up and stored in an easily accessible format that can be used during outages. Training staff on emergency protocols and temporary measures to manage network operations without full access to records is also essential.

Ethical and Legal Considerations

In considering the feasibility of manual operations, ethical and legal questions arise. Can a telecom company ethically or legally stop operations until technology is restored? What are the implications for customers relying on continuous telecom services? These questions highlight the importance of robust contingency plans that ensure continuity of network operations even during technology outages. While it is understood that a telecom company may not have ethical and legal issues as big as the hospitals and banks and pharma companies may have.

Conclusion

This discussion remains inconclusive. The transition from paper to digital systems was driven by the need for efficiency and accuracy in network operations. However, when technology fails, access to records is disrupted, making backups ineffective. Resorting to manual operations and paper records is impractical unless they are created simultaneously with digital entries, which is unreasonable.

Therefore, it is essential to set realistic expectations not only for telecom companies but also for their customers and stakeholders. While resilient IT systems can significantly reduce downtime, it cannot be entirely avoided. Both providers and beneficiaries must understand that certain situations will necessitate living with temporary downtimes. The focus should be on minimizing these periods through robust IT disaster recovery plans and ensuring that staff are prepared to manage network operations effectively during these outages. Setting appropriate expectations is key to navigating these challenges without making bold claims about the infallibility of IT systems.

5.   Aviation: Flight Operations Process During Technology Failures

Introduction

In the aviation sector, flight operations rely heavily on advanced technology systems for scheduling, navigation, communication, and safety management. These systems ensure the efficient and safe operation of flights across the globe. This article explores the current process of technology-based flight operations, the feasibility of reverting to manual operations during technological outages, and the challenges and risks associated with such a transition.

Current Process and Dependencies

The assumption underlying this analysis is that flight operations are fully managed using advanced technology systems. These systems handle scheduling, air traffic control (ATC), navigation, communication, weather monitoring, and safety management. The efficiency of these systems relies on various technologies, including hardware (radars, communication devices), software (flight management systems), and third-party services (satellite navigation, weather forecasting). Additionally, skilled IT and aviation personnel are necessary to maintain and troubleshoot these systems.

Steps for Manual Operation

In the event of a technology failure, aviation companies might consider transitioning to manual operations. However, the feasibility of manual flight operations is highly questionable. The steps for manual flight operations would involve:

1.   Manual Scheduling: Coordinating flight schedules using phone calls, written logs, and physical charts.

2.   Manual Air Traffic Control: Using visual signals, radio communication, and physical coordination between pilots and ground staff.

3.   Manual Navigation: Pilots relying on traditional navigation methods such as visual flight rules (VFR) and manual compass navigation.

4.   Manual Communication: Relaying information through radio communication without digital aids.

5.   Manual Weather Monitoring: Using local weather observations and reports instead of real-time digital weather data.

6.   Manual Safety Management: Ensuring safety protocols are followed through physical inspections and checklists.

Challenges and Risks of Manual Operations

The feasibility of manual flight operations is extremely limited due to numerous challenges and risks:

- Safety Concerns: The primary concern is safety. Without technology, the risk of accidents and incidents increases significantly.

- Lack of Real-Time Data: Inability to access real-time data for navigation, weather, and traffic management, leading to potential hazards.

- Human Error: Increased risk of inaccuracies in scheduling, navigation, communication, and safety protocols due to manual handling.

- Coordination Challenges: Difficulty in coordinating actions between different airports, air traffic control centers, and aircraft, potentially leading to delays and miscommunication.

- Time-Consuming: Significantly more time required for all operations, leading to delays and inefficiencies.

- Data Sharing: Difficulty in sharing information between different stakeholders, potentially leading to miscommunication and operational issues.

- Reintegration into Digital Systems: The necessity to digitize all manually recorded information once the technology is restored, which can be labor-intensive and prone to errors.

Feasibility Analysis

I realized that there is zero feasibility of flight operations being done manually, so this case may appear to be ending abruptly.

1. Flight Scheduling and Planning

    o Technology Role: Flight scheduling involves complex algorithms to manage aircraft rotations, crew schedules, maintenance requirements, and airport slots.

    o Manual Feasibility: Manual scheduling would be incredibly time-consuming and prone to errors, making it impractical.

2. Air Traffic Control (ATC)

    o Technology Role: ATC relies on radar, communication systems, and real-time data to manage aircraft movements safely and efficiently.

    o Manual Feasibility: Manual air traffic control would be extremely risky, as visual methods and basic radio communication are insufficient for managing high volumes of air traffic.

3. Navigation and Communication

    o Technology Role: Aircraft navigation systems use GPS, onboard computers, and automated systems to ensure precise routing and safety.

    o Manual Feasibility: Manual navigation using traditional methods like maps and compasses would be highly impractical and unsafe, especially for commercial flights.

4. Weather Monitoring

    o Technology Role: Real-time weather data is crucial for flight planning and safety. Technology provides constant updates on weather conditions along flight routes.

    o Manual Feasibility: Manual weather monitoring lacks the precision and timeliness needed for safe flight operations.

5. Safety Management

    o Technology Role: Safety protocols are enforced through automated systems that monitor aircraft systems, pilot actions, and external conditions.

    o Manual Feasibility: Manual safety management would not provide the same level of oversight and immediate response capabilities.

Recent Airline Disruptions: When technology systems fail, airlines experience significant disruptions. For instance, the issuance of manual boarding passes can help manage the passenger flow to some extent, but the check-in process, baggage handling, and flight operations still depend heavily on functioning IT systems. During such outages, flights are often delayed or canceled until systems are restored.

Conclusion

In the context of aviation, manual operations are not a viable alternative for the following reasons:

- Safety Risks: The primary concern is safety. Aviation operations rely on precise, real-time data and automated systems to ensure the safety of flights. Manual operations cannot provide the same level of safety.

- Operational Complexity: The complexity of coordinating flight schedules, air traffic, navigation, and communication exceeds what can be managed manually.

- Efficiency Loss: Manual operations would be significantly slower, leading to delays and inefficiencies that would ripple throughout the entire airline network.

- Regulatory Compliance: Aviation regulations mandate the use of specific technologies to ensure safety and efficiency. Operating without these technologies would not meet regulatory standards.

Setting and managing expectations is crucial, even in the aviation sector. Here is how setting appropriate expectations and managing them can help mitigate the impact of technology failures:

Communication with Passengers

- Transparency: Clear communication about the nature and duration of disruptions can help manage passenger expectations. Informing passengers about the steps being taken to resolve the issue and providing regular updates can reduce frustration and confusion.

- Alternative Arrangements: Providing information about alternative arrangements, such as rebooking on different flights or offering accommodation, helps manage expectations and provides a sense of control to the passengers.

Staff Training and Preparedness

- Emergency Protocols: Training staff to handle situations when technology fails ensures that they can manage operations manually to the extent possible and maintain safety and order.

- Customer Service: Equipping customer service staff with the tools and information to handle passenger inquiries and concerns can alleviate stress and maintain trust.

Redundant Systems and Backups

- IT Resilience: Implementing redundant systems and robust IT infrastructure minimizes the risk of complete outages. Regular testing and maintenance of these systems are essential to ensure they function correctly when needed.

- Data Backup: Ensuring critical data is backed up and accessible even during outages helps maintain some level of operational capability.

- In a case like Crowdstrike incident where the frontend failed while backend was all ok – no contingency/ resilience/ business continuity arrangements would have worked. Yes, it's worth exploring whether those backend systems/ information could be accessed through smartphones and to what extent. Ther displays at the airports were still operational to show delayed and cancelled flights – so perhaps some such devices like phones were integrated with the systems and did work to whatever extent.

Setting Realistic Expectations

- Public Awareness: Educating the public about the complexities of aviation operations and the potential for disruptions can set realistic expectations. Highlighting the industry's commitment to safety and the measures in place to handle emergencies can foster understanding.

- Acknowledging Limitations: Being honest about the limitations of manual operations and the potential delays or cancellations that might result from technology failures can help set realistic expectations.

Conclusion

While the aviation sector's reliance on technology makes manual operations largely impractical for core functions, setting and managing expectations appropriately remains vital. Clear communication, staff preparedness, resilient IT systems, and continuous improvement efforts can help mitigate the impact of technology failures. By setting realistic expectations and being transparent with passengers, the aviation industry can maintain trust and ensure safety even during disruptions.

6. Government: Citizen Services Process During Technology Failures

Introduction

In government services, the management and delivery of citizen services rely heavily on advanced technology systems. These systems facilitate the digital entry, storage, and retrieval of citizen information, ensuring seamless service delivery. This article explores the current process of technology-based citizen services management, the feasibility of reverting to manual operations during technological outages, and the challenges and risks associated with such a transition.

Current Process and Dependencies

The assumption underlying this analysis is that citizen services are fully managed using advanced technology systems. These systems handle everything from application processing and service delivery to records management and communication. The efficiency of these systems relies on various technologies, including hardware (servers, computers), software (management systems), and third-party services (cloud services, cybersecurity). Additionally, skilled IT personnel are necessary to maintain and troubleshoot these systems.

Steps for Manual Operation

In the event of a technology failure, government agencies might consider transitioning to manual operations. The steps for manual citizen services management would involve:

1. **Application Processing on Paper**: Collecting and processing applications using physical forms and manual entry.

2. **Service Delivery Manually**: Providing services through in-person interactions and written records.

3. **Records Management and Communication**: Managing records and communicating with citizens manually using written records and phone calls.

Challenges and Risks of Manual Operations

Despite the feasibility of manual operations, several challenges and risks emerge:

- **Lack of Real-Time Data**: Without access to digital systems, real-time tracking and management of services is impossible, leading to potential delays and inefficiencies.

- **Human Error**: Increased risk of inaccuracies in data entry, processing, and communication due to manual handling.

- **Time-Consuming**: Significantly more time required for processing applications, delivering services, and managing records compared to automated systems.

- **Coordination Challenges**: Difficulty in coordinating actions between different departments and locations, potentially leading to delays in response.

- **Data Sharing**: Difficulty in sharing information between different departments and partners, potentially leading to miscommunication and inefficiencies.

- **Reintegration into Digital Systems**: The necessity to digitize all manually recorded information once the technology is restored, which can be labor-intensive and prone to errors.

Feasibility Analysis

While manual citizen services management is feasible, it is highly inefficient and filled with risks. The primary concerns include the risk of human error, time consumption, coordination challenges, and the burden of reintegrating data into digital systems. Food for Thought:

- Most services provided by the government agencies may fall under 'non-critical' – if they would have conducted any BIA.

- Its not only that the government agency will resort to manual/ paper based responses, even the citizens will need to request services in manual/ paper base mode – and those forms may not be available/ not available easily.

So, this is a non-starter for such processes and services.

Recommendations

Given the constraints of manual operations, it may be more practical for government agencies to focus on minimizing downtime through robust IT disaster recovery plans and ensuring quick restoration of citizen services management systems. Critical citizen information should be regularly backed up and stored in an easily accessible format that can be used during outages. Training staff on emergency protocols and temporary measures to manage citizen services without full access to records is also essential.

Ethical and Legal Considerations

In considering the feasibility of manual operations, ethical and legal questions arise. Can a government agency ethically or legally stop services until technology is restored? What are the implications for citizens relying on continuous services? These questions highlight the importance of robust contingency plans that ensure continuity of citizen services even during technology outages. Do they sign any contracts with the citizens? Do they have any legal/ contractual/ ethical liabilities?

Conclusion

This discussion remains inconclusive. The transition from paper to digital systems was driven by the need for efficiency and accuracy in citizen services management. However, when technology fails, access to records is disrupted, making backups ineffective. Resorting to paper records is impractical unless they are created simultaneously with digital entries, which is unreasonable.

Therefore, it is essential to set realistic expectations not only for government agencies but also for citizens and stakeholders. While resilient IT systems can significantly reduce downtime, it cannot be entirely avoided. Both providers and beneficiaries must understand that certain situations will necessitate living with temporary downtimes. The focus should be on minimizing these periods through robust IT disaster recovery plans and ensuring that staff are prepared to manage citizen services effectively during these outages. Setting appropriate expectations is key to navigating these challenges without making bold claims about the infallibility of IT systems.

The case may be that the government services will be stopped during technological failure (again of the type of Crowdstrike events – else the ITDR/ Resilience/ BC Arrangements will cover – if any).

7.   **Education: Student Records Management Process During Technology Failures**

Introduction

In the education sector, student records management relies heavily on advanced technology systems. These systems facilitate the digital entry, storage, and retrieval of student information, ensuring seamless academic administration. This article explores the current process of technology-based student records management, the feasibility of reverting to manual operations during technological outages, and the challenges and risks associated with such a transition.

Current Process and Dependencies

The assumption underlying this analysis is that student records management is fully managed using advanced technology systems. These systems handle everything from application processing and record keeping to communication, lectures and exams scheduling, exam processing and reporting. The efficiency of these systems relies on various technologies, including hardware (servers, computers), software (management systems), and third-party services (cloud services, cybersecurity). Additionally, skilled IT personnel are necessary to maintain and troubleshoot these systems.

Steps for Manual Operation

In the event of a technology failure, educational institutions might consider transitioning to manual operations. The steps for manual student records management would involve:

1.   **Application Processing on Paper**: Collecting and processing student applications using physical forms and manual entry, including fee collection/ processing.

2.   **Record Keeping Manually**: Maintaining student records through written logs and physical files.

3.   **Communication and Reporting**: Communicating with students and generating reports manually using written records and phone calls.

4.   **Lectures and Exams Scheduling**: Scheduling lectures and exams manually, including keeping the records

5.   **Exam Processing**: Processing exams manually. Needing solved papers as well as master answers.

Challenges and Risks of Manual Operations

Despite the feasibility of manual operations, several challenges and risks emerge:

- **Lack of Real-Time Data**: Without access to digital systems, real-time tracking and management of student information is impossible, leading to potential delays and inefficiencies.

- **Human Error**: Increased risk of inaccuracies in data entry, record keeping, and communication due to manual handling.

- **Time-Consuming**: Significantly more time required for processing applications, maintaining records, and generating reports compared to automated systems.

- **Coordination Challenges**: Difficulty in coordinating actions between different departments and locations, potentially leading to delays in response.

- **Data Sharing**: Difficulty in sharing information between different departments and partners, potentially leading to miscommunication and inefficiencies.

- **Reintegration into Digital Systems**: The necessity to digitize all manually recorded information once the technology is restored, which can be labor-intensive and prone to errors.

Feasibility Analysis

While manual student records management is feasible, it is highly inefficient and filled with risks. The primary concerns include the risk of human error, time consumption, coordination challenges, and the burden of reintegrating data into digital systems.

Recommendations

Given the constraints of manual operations, it may be more practical for educational institutions to focus on minimizing downtime through robust IT disaster recovery plans and ensuring quick restoration of student records management systems. Critical student information should be regularly backed up and stored in an easily accessible format that can be used during outages. Training staff on emergency protocols and temporary measures to manage student records without full access to records is also essential.

Ethical and Legal Considerations

In considering the feasibility of manual operations, ethical and legal questions arise. Can an educational institution ethically or legally stop services until technology is restored? What are the implications for students relying on continuous academic administration? These questions highlight the importance of robust contingency plans that ensure continuity of student records management even during technology outages.

Conclusion

Most processes in the education sector related to student record management can be done manually easily.

Student record keeping in the education sector, while important, does not carry the same level of criticality as operations in sectors like healthcare or aviation. Short-term disruptions can generally be managed with manual processes, and the impact on students and administrative functions is typically minimal. Setting and managing expectations and clear and effective communication will be key, when the work may better be stopped for hours or days, if required.

8. Insurance: Claims Process During Technology Failures

Introduction

In the insurance industry, claims processing relies heavily on advanced technology systems. These systems facilitate the digital entry, assessment, and settlement of claims, ensuring timely and accurate service delivery. This article explores the current process of technology-based claims processing, the feasibility of reverting to manual operations during technological outages, and the challenges and risks associated with such a transition.

Current Process and Dependencies

The assumption underlying this analysis is that claims processing is fully managed using advanced technology systems. These systems handle everything from claims submission and assessment to communication and settlement. The efficiency of these systems relies on various technologies, including hardware (servers, computers), software (claims management systems), and third-party services (cloud services, cybersecurity). Additionally, skilled IT personnel are necessary to maintain and troubleshoot these systems.

Steps for Manual Operation

In the event of a technology failure, insurance companies might consider transitioning to manual operations. The steps for manual claims processing would involve:

1. **Claims Submission on Paper**: Collecting claims using physical forms and manual entry.

2. **Claims Assessment and Settlement Manually**: Assessing and settling claims through written records and manual calculations.

3. **Communication and Reporting**: Communicating with claimants and generating reports manually using written records and phone calls.

Challenges and Risks of Manual Operations

Despite the feasibility of manual operations, several challenges and risks emerge:

- **Lack of Real-Time Data**: Without access to digital systems, real-time tracking and management of claims is impossible, leading to potential delays and inefficiencies.

- **Human Error**: Increased risk of inaccuracies in data entry, assessment, and communication due to manual handling.

- **Time-Consuming**: Significantly more time required for processing claims, assessing information, and generating reports compared to automated systems.

- **Coordination Challenges**: Difficulty in coordinating actions between different departments and locations, potentially leading to delays in response.

- **Data Sharing**: Difficulty in sharing information between different departments and partners, potentially leading to miscommunication and inefficiencies.

- **Reintegration into Digital Systems**: The necessity to digitize all manually recorded information once the technology is restored, which can be labor-intensive and prone to errors.

Additionally:

- **Complexity and Volume of Data:**

  - **Policy Details**: Insurance claims processing requires access to detailed policy information, including policyholder names, policy numbers, coverage details, and the policy status. These details are stored digitally and are not typically printed or maintained in hard copy on a daily basis.

  - **Verification**: Manual verification of claims would be extremely time-consuming and prone to errors without access to up-to-date digital records.

- **Efficiency and Accuracy:**

  - **Data Entry Errors:** Manually processing claims increases the likelihood of errors in data entry and verification, which can lead to incorrect claim approvals or rejections.

  - **Processing Time:** The time required to manually process each claim would significantly delay the overall claims process, impacting customer satisfaction and trust.

- **Security and Privacy:**

  - **Sensitive Information:** Claims processing involves handling sensitive and personal information. Ensuring the security and privacy of this information is challenging in a manual system.

  - **Data Breaches:** Manual handling increases the risk of data breaches and loss of sensitive information.

- **Lack of Infrastructure:**

  - **Physical Records:** Most insurance companies do not maintain physical copies of all records. Transitioning to a manual process would require creating and maintaining extensive physical records, which is not practical.

Feasibility of Accepting Downtime

Given the impracticality of manual operations, a more feasible approach is to accept limited downtime and focus on restoring digital systems quickly. Here are some considerations:

1. **Service Level Agreements (SLAs):**

   - **Non-Immediate Processing:** Insurance claims typically have SLAs that allow for processing times of several days. A short-term outage of a few hours to a day or two can generally be accommodated within these SLAs without significant impact on service levels.

   - **Communication:** Clear communication with policyholders about expected delays and the steps being taken to resolve the issue can help manage expectations.

2. **Prioritizing Critical Claims:**

   - **Life Insurance Claims:** While all claims are important, life insurance claims are particularly sensitive due to the emotional and financial impact on beneficiaries. Prioritizing the resolution of these claims once systems are restored can help mitigate the impact of downtime.

3. **IT Resilience and Disaster Recovery:**

   - **Redundancy and Backups:** Ensuring that robust IT infrastructure, including redundant systems and regular backups, is in place can minimize the risk of extended outages.

   - **Rapid Response:** Having a well-defined disaster recovery plan and trained IT personnel to quickly address and resolve system failures is crucial.

Conclusion

Manual processing of insurance claims is not feasible due to the complexity, volume of data, and need for accuracy and security. Accepting limited downtime and focusing on rapid restoration of digital systems is a more practical approach. Insurance companies should communicate effectively with policyholders about delays and prioritize critical claims, particularly life insurance claims, once systems are back online. By setting realistic expectations and having robust IT resilience plans, insurance companies can manage the impact of technology failures while maintaining trust and customer satisfaction.

9.   Real Estate: Property Management Process During Technology Failures

Introduction

In the real estate industry, property management relies heavily on advanced technology systems. These systems facilitate the digital entry, storage, and retrieval of property information, ensuring seamless management and communication. This article explores the current process of technology-based property management, the feasibility of reverting to manual operations during technological outages, and the challenges and risks associated with such a transition.

Current Process and Dependencies

The assumption underlying this analysis is that property management is fully managed using advanced technology systems. These systems handle everything from tenant applications and lease management to maintenance requests and communication. The efficiency of these systems relies on various technologies, including hardware (servers, computers), software (property management systems), and third-party services (cloud services, cybersecurity). Additionally, skilled IT personnel are necessary to maintain and troubleshoot these systems.

Steps for Manual Operation

In the event of a technology failure, property management companies might consider transitioning to manual operations. The steps for manual property management would involve:

1. **Tenant Applications on Paper**: Collecting and processing tenant applications using physical forms and manual entry.

2. **Lease Management and Maintenance Requests Manually**: Managing leases and maintenance requests through written records and physical files.

3. **Communication and Reporting**: Communicating with tenants and generating reports manually using written records and phone calls.

Challenges and Risks of Manual Operations

Despite the feasibility of manual operations, several challenges and risks emerge:

- **Lack of Real-Time Data**: Without access to digital systems, real-time tracking and management of property information is impossible, leading to potential delays and inefficiencies.

- **Human Error**: Increased risk of inaccuracies in data entry, lease management, and communication due to manual handling.

- **Time-Consuming**: Significantly more time required for processing applications, managing leases, and generating reports compared to automated systems.

- **Coordination Challenges**: Difficulty in coordinating actions between different departments and locations, potentially leading to delays in response.

- **Data Sharing**: Difficulty in sharing information between different departments and partners, potentially leading to miscommunication and inefficiencies.

- **Reintegration into Digital Systems**: The necessity to digitize all manually recorded information once the technology is restored, which can be labor-intensive and prone to errors.

Feasibility Analysis

A portion of property management i.e. maintenance can most easily be transitioned to manual/ paper mode – this does not generally depend upon historical data. The rest of the process may be highly inefficient and filled with risks if transitioned to manual mode. The primary concerns include the risk of human error, time consumption, coordination challenges, and the burden of reintegrating data into digital systems.

Recommendations

Given the constraints of manual operations, it may be more practical for property management companies to focus on minimizing downtime through robust IT disaster recovery plans and ensuring quick restoration of property management systems. Critical property information should be regularly backed up and stored in an easily accessible format that can be used during outages. Training staff on emergency protocols and temporary measures to manage property information without full access to records is also essential. A portion of the process i.e. maintenance can easily be transitioned to manual mode and even the re-entry of the information into the systems (when the technology is up) will be easier as this is a simpler information too.

Ethical and Legal Considerations

In considering the feasibility of manual operations, ethical and legal questions arise. Can a property management company ethically or legally stop services until technology is restored? What are the implications for tenants relying on continuous property management services? These questions highlight the importance of robust contingency plans that ensure continuity of property management even during technology outages. The answer may be no to having any ethical or legal issues in the property management process in the real estate sector.

Conclusion

This discussion is more conclusive than many. The transition from paper to digital systems was driven by the need for efficiency and accuracy in property management. However, when technology fails, access to records is disrupted, making backups ineffective. Resorting to paper records is impractical unless they are created simultaneously with digital entries, which is unreasonable.

Therefore, it is essential to set realistic expectations not only for property management companies but also for their tenants and stakeholders. While resilient IT systems can significantly reduce downtime, it cannot be entirely avoided. Both providers and beneficiaries must understand that certain situations will necessitate living with temporary downtimes. The focus should be on minimizing these periods through robust IT disaster recovery plans and ensuring that staff are prepared to manage property information effectively during these outages. Setting appropriate expectations is key to navigating these challenges without making bold claims about the infallibility of IT systems.

10. All Industries: Visitor Management Process During Technology Failures

Introduction

In modern organizations, visitor management (including regular staff, contractors etc.) is a crucial process to ensure security, track visitor activity, and maintain a professional environment. Electronic visitor management systems (EVMS) facilitate the digital entry, storage, and retrieval of visitor information, ensuring efficient and secure handling of visitors. However, the dependency on technology raises the question: what happens when these systems fail? This article explores the current process of EVMS-based visitor management, the feasibility of reverting to manual operations during technological outages, and the challenges and risks associated with such a transition.

Current Process and Dependencies

The assumption underlying this analysis is that visitor management is fully managed using EVMS. This digital process includes the entry, storage, and retrieval of visitor information, with seamless sharing between security personnel and relevant departments. The efficiency of EVMS relies on various technologies, including hardware (computers, servers), software (visitor management systems), and third-party services (cloud storage, cybersecurity services). Additionally, skilled IT personnel are necessary to maintain and troubleshoot these systems.

Steps for Manual Operation

In the event of a technology failure, organizations might consider transitioning to manual operations. The steps for manual visitor management would involve:

1. **Manual Sign-In/Sign-Out**: Visitors sign in and out using paper logbooks, capturing essential details such as name, contact information, time of entry, purpose of visit, and host.

2. **Identification and Badges**: Issue temporary visitor badges manually, noting the details in the logbook. Ensure that badges are clearly marked to distinguish visitors from employees.

3. **Security Checks**: Security personnel manually verify visitor identities using government-issued IDs and conduct bag checks if necessary.

4. **Notification to Hosts**: Use phone calls or internal messaging systems to inform hosts about their visitors.

Challenges and Risks of Manual Operations

Despite the feasibility of manual operations, several challenges and risks emerge:

- **Accuracy and Legibility**: Increased risk of errors in data entry, such as incorrect names or times, which can affect record accuracy. Handwritten entries may be difficult to read or interpret.

- **Data Management**: Storing and retrieving paper logs can be cumbersome, and finding specific entries may take time. Physical records are at risk of being lost, damaged, or stolen.

- **Security and Compliance**: Manual processes can slow down visitor processing, leading to longer wait times and potential security lapses. Ensuring compliance with regulatory requirements may be challenging without digital systems to automatically log and track visitor data.

- **Efficiency**: The manual process is less efficient, leading to longer processing times and potential frustration for visitors and staff.

Feasibility Analysis

While manual visitor management is feasible, it is highly inefficient and filled with risks. The primary concerns include the risk of human error, time consumption, storage and security issues, and the burden of managing paper records. Additionally, the lack of access to digital records and the manual notification process are significant barriers.

Recommendations

Given the constraints of manual operations, it may be more practical for organizations to focus on minimizing downtime through robust IT disaster recovery plans and ensuring quick restoration of EVMS. Here are some recommendations:

- **Redundancy and Backups**: Implement robust IT infrastructure, including redundant systems and regular backups, to minimize the risk of extended outages.

- **Temporary Measures**: Simplify the manual process as much as possible to minimize delays and errors. Deploy additional staff to assist with the manual process and ensure smooth operations.

- **Training**: Train security personnel on emergency protocols and temporary measures to manage visitor processing during outages.

- **Communication**: Clearly communicate the temporary manual process to staff and visitors, explaining the reason for the change and any expected delays.

Ethical and Legal Considerations

In considering the feasibility of manual operations, ethical and legal questions arise. Can an organization ethically or legally stop visitor processing until technology is restored? Can they refuse entry to visitors due to technological failures? These questions highlight the importance of robust contingency plans that ensure continuity of operations even during technology outages.

Conclusion

Visitor management is an important process for ensuring security and maintaining a professional environment. While it may not be as critical as other operational processes, it is still essential for organizations. In the event of a technology failure, transitioning to manual operations is feasible but comes with challenges related to accuracy, efficiency, and compliance. Setting appropriate expectations and focusing on quick IT recovery can help manage the impact of such disruptions. Both organizations and visitors must understand that certain situations will necessitate living with temporary downtimes. The focus should be on minimizing these periods through robust IT disaster recovery plans and ensuring that staff are prepared to manage visitor processing effectively during these outages.

From all the picked up processes in this chapter, this one is common to all industries, while criticality may vary. Also, it's easiest to be transitioned to manual. paper mode. This is also least dependent on the historical data in the immediate sense. While many other processes may stopped for hours or days, visitor management immediately impacts the entry of staff (exit may be delayed, no challenge) which has direct impact on the work output. Entry portion becomes more critical from security point of view (anti-social elements/ terrorists may enter), the Exit portion becomes more important if an evacuation is required during such technology failure times when information about those needing help in evacuation may not be available (e.g. who are physical challenged or who are pregnant ladies in the office).

Final words: Feasibility of Manual Operations Across Different Sectors During Technology Failures

The reliance on technology has transformed the efficiency and accuracy of operations across various sectors. From healthcare and aviation to utilities and insurance, technology plays a crucial role in ensuring seamless operations. However, the potential for technology failures raises the question of whether manual operations can serve as a viable backup. My exploration of ten sectors reveals diverse perspectives on the feasibility, challenges, and implications of reverting to manual processes.

General Feasibility of Manual Operations

Across most sectors, transitioning to manual operations is theoretically feasible but often impractical and full of challenges. Manual processes generally introduce significant inefficiencies, increase the risk of errors, and pose substantial logistical and security challenges. For instance:

- **Healthcare**: While it is possible to manage patient records manually, the process is highly inefficient and prone to errors, particularly in emergencies where access to historical data is crucial.

- **Utilities**: Manual monitoring and load balancing are theoretically feasible, but calibration and the reliance on historical data for grid management make this approach highly impractical and risky.

- **Aviation**: The complexity of flight operations, reliance on real-time data, and stringent safety requirements make manual operations largely infeasible. Limited manual operations, such as issuing boarding passes, can be performed, but overall flight operations depend on robust IT systems.

- **Education**: Manual student record-keeping can be temporarily managed with minimal risk, making this sector less critical compared to others.

- **Insurance**: Manual claims processing is highly impractical due to the need for accurate policy verification and risk of errors. Delays in processing are more acceptable than the risks introduced by manual handling.

Sector-Specific Insights

Each sector presents unique challenges and considerations:

1. **Healthcare**: Critical need for quick restoration of EHR systems and robust IT disaster recovery plans to minimize downtime and ensure patient safety.

2. **Utilities**: Importance of maintaining accurate and calibrated monitoring systems and the impracticality of manual grid management.

3. **Telecom**: Dependence on real-time data and the complexity of network management make manual operations challenging, but temporary measures can be implemented.

4. **Aviation**: Essential reliance on IT systems for safety and efficiency; limited manual operations feasible but insufficient for overall functionality.

5. **Government**: The feasibility of manual processes varies by department, with critical services requiring quick IT restoration.

6. **Education**: Less critical, with manual processes feasible for short durations without significant risk.

7. **Insurance**: Emphasis on ensuring accurate claims processing and the importance of maintaining digital records.

8. **Real Estate**: Manual processes are feasible but less efficient; reliance on digital systems for accurate data management is preferred.

9. **Pharmaceuticals**: Critical need for accurate data management and compliance with regulations; manual operations introduce significant risks.

10. **Visitor Management in Corporates**: Feasible but inefficient; quick restoration of EVMS is preferred for maintaining security and efficiency.

Ethical and Legal Considerations

Across all sectors, ethical and legal considerations play a significant role. Organizations must balance the need to continue operations with the potential risks introduced by manual processes. In critical sectors like healthcare and aviation, the inability to provide services due to technological failures raises significant ethical and legal questions. Ensuring robust IT disaster recovery plans and setting realistic expectations for both providers and beneficiaries is crucial. But I admit that I could not put enough emphasis as I did not have knowledge about such requirements of each industry.

Recommendations

Based on my analysis, the following recommendations are vital for managing technology failures:

1. **Robust IT Disaster Recovery Plans**: Invest in comprehensive IT disaster recovery and business continuity plans to minimize downtime and ensure quick restoration of services.

2. **Training and Preparedness**: Train staff on emergency protocols and temporary measures to manage operations during outages effectively.

3. **Communication**: Clearly communicate the limitations and expected downtimes to stakeholders, including staff, customers, and beneficiaries.

4. **Regular Backups**: Implement regular backups of critical data and ensure that some information is accessible in a format that can be used during outages.

5. **Redundancy and Resilience**: Enhance IT infrastructure with redundant systems and resilience measures to prevent extended disruptions.

While closing, I must mention that all IT DR, Resilience, Business Continuity arrangements would not work in certain cases like Crowdstrike type incidents where access to IT/ Information/ Records was interrupted by the frontend arrangements while the backend arrangements were intact. 'Going to manual operations and paper based mode' has been said to be a workaround in such cases but that is highly impractical, not feasible as a main requirement would be to keep all data/ information/ records on paper also during BAU (business as usual) itself. This is not doable!

Guest Chapter 1: The Resilient Indian Economy in Light of Payment Digitisation

Tanuj Sood
System Engineer C1 with the major IT Company, India

The question of imposing fees on Unified Payments Interface (UPI) transactions is a hot topic of debate today. To arrive at a well-informed decision, it is essential to examine the facts and figures surrounding UPI and the third-party stakeholders involved in these transactions. UPI has become the backbone of India's digital payments ecosystem, serving everyone from the largest corporates and e-commerce platforms to local panwalas, vegetable vendors, and even cobblers on the street.

With over **14.96 billion transactions a month** and more than **350 million active users** as of August 2024, UPI's reach spans both urban and rural India. From conglomerates like **Reliance** and **Tata**, which use UPI to facilitate seamless B2C payments, to small business owners and micro-entrepreneurs who rely on the platform for day-to-day sales, UPI has democratized digital payments. **Street vendors, kirana stores, and even taxi drivers** use UPI, making it a critical tool for financial inclusion.

The introduction of transaction fees could affect these users differently. Small vendors and daily-wage workers, who rely heavily on low-cost or free digital payments, may shift back to cash if fees are imposed, disrupting their newly found digital convenience. Corporates and larger businesses might absorb the cost, but the decline in overall digital transactions could have a cascading effect on fintech companies, banks, and payment service providers that facilitate these UPI payments.

This potential decline could also hurt the broader Indian economy, which has increasingly benefited from the shift to a cashless system, reducing black money circulation and enhancing transparency. The ripple effects on various industries, financial services, and the informal economy need careful consideration as UPI supports a vast spectrum of economic activity, from small-scale to large-scale operations. Therefore, any policy decisions regarding UPI fees should account for the diverse user base and the economic implications of disrupting this thriving digital payments ecosystem.

The third parties involved in the functioning of UPI transactions are-

1. National Payments Corporation of India (NPCI)

NPCI is the central entity that manages and operates the UPI platform. It oversees all technical operations, regulatory compliance, settlement between banks, and transaction validation. Also, NPCI provides the base IT infrastructure.

2. Banks (PSPs and Issuer Banks)

Payment Service Providers (PSPs): Banks act as PSPs that provide the infrastructure to connect to the UPI system and enable transactions. They are responsible for hosting UPI services and ensuring seamless integration with NPCI's UPI infrastructure.

Issuer Banks: These are the banks where users hold their accounts. They participate in UPI by linking customer bank accounts to the UPI network, handling transaction processing, and ensuring security.

Example- Bank of Baroda, State Bank of India

3. Reserve Bank of India (RBI)

The RBI acts as the primary regulator of the payments system in India. It provides oversight, ensures compliance with the banking regulations, and supports financial inclusion initiatives through the UPI framework.

4. Payment Aggregators

These are entities that facilitate the flow of funds between customers and merchants. They provide merchant services for businesses to accept UPI payments without directly interacting with multiple banks.

Example: One of the most well-known payment aggregators in India is **Razorpay**. It allows businesses, from large enterprises to small merchants, to accept UPI payments alongside other modes of payment, streamlining the process for both the merchant and the customer.

5. Merchants

Merchants (both online and offline) accept UPI payments from customers. They play a crucial role in UPI's adoption as they integrate UPI as a mode of payment for their services and products.

6. Third-Party Payment Service Providers (TPPSP)

These are non-bank entities that facilitate UPI transactions by offering UPI-based services. Examples include tech companies and payment facilitators like Google Pay and PhonePe. While not third-party apps, they work with partner banks to process UPI payments.

7. Authentication Providers

Authentication providers, such as those offering Aadhaar-based biometric verification or mobile number OTP-based authentication, ensure secure validation of users during transactions. They work with UPI to verify identities and approve transactions securely.

Example- Digilocker for Aadhaar verification etc.

8. NPCI Infrastructure Partners

These partners assist in the operational infrastructure, including data centers, cloud service providers, and cybersecurity firms, which help NPCI manage UPI's backend and security frameworks.

There are approximately 1.6 to 2.2 million direct and indirect jobs across all the third parties in the UPI ecosystem. The number could vary based on specific roles and the growth of digital payment adoption in India.

The estimate of **1.6 to 2.2 million direct and indirect jobs** in the UPI ecosystem is based on industry reports and analyses from **NPCI (National Payments Corporation of India)**, **RBI** annual reports, and market research from organizations such as **BCG** and **NASSCOM**.

Decline in UPI (digital) payments if any transaction fee is imposed is a risk on these direct or indirect jobs.

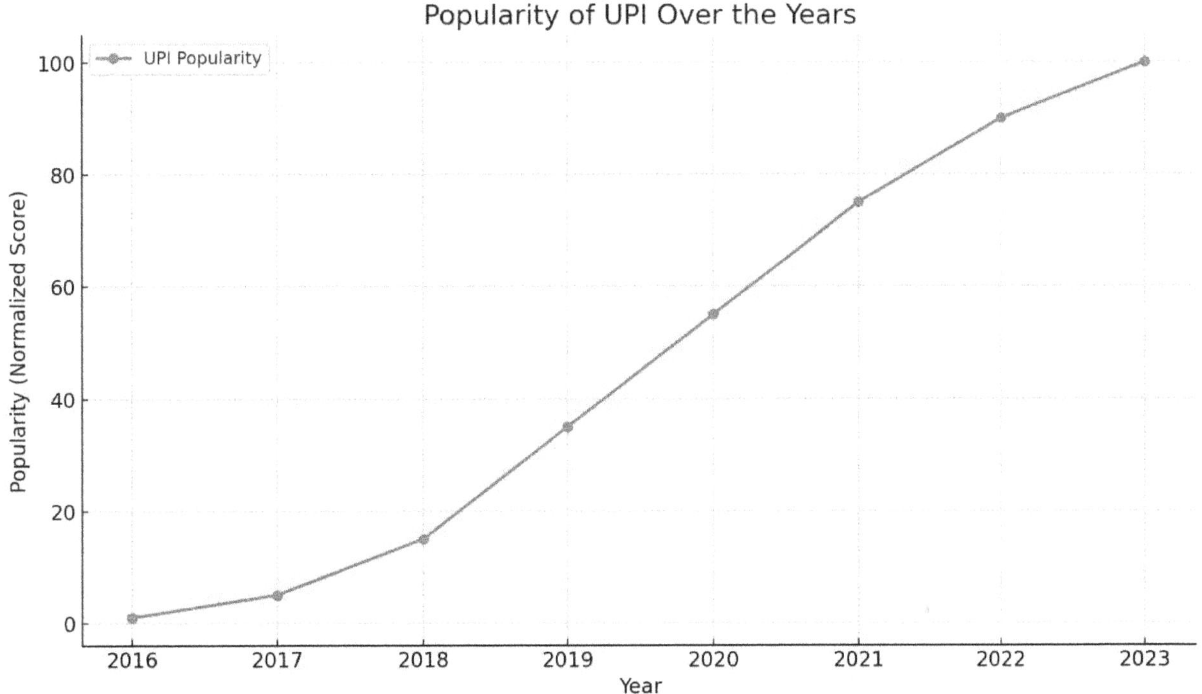

Further, let us look onto some statistics of the UPI since its inception-

Monthly and Annual UPI Transactions:

UPI started with very low transaction volumes in 2016. The monthly transactions have steadily increased, and as of August 2024, UPI transactions have surged to 14.96 billion per month, reflecting a 41% year-on-year increase. This marks a significant rise compared to previous years, with UPI now handling more than ₹20 lakh crore worth of transactions each month.

The annual transaction count has also surged from 12 million in 2016 to around 108 billion transactions annually in 2023.

Source – data collected from official NPCI website and graph plotted using matplotlib in python.

Popularity Growth:

UPI's popularity has grown exponentially, especially from 2018 onward. The graph shows a significant rise in its usage and acceptance, achieving a peak popularity score of 100 by 2024, reflecting widespread adoption and integration into daily life.

Levying a fee on UPI transactions could have several potential impacts on transaction volume, user behaviour, and the overall popularity of UPI.

Below is a breakdown of these impacts, followed by an approach to visualize the possible outcomes through comparative graphs.

Levying a fee on UPI transactions could generate significant revenue for the government, contributing to national development:

1 paisa per transaction: With 15 billion monthly transactions, this could bring in ₹1.8 billion per year.

10 paisa per transaction: The revenue could rise to ₹18 billion annually.

₹1 per transaction: The government could generate ₹180 billion annually.

These funds could be used for infrastructure projects, education, healthcare, and boosting digital inclusion, improving overall economic growth. However, there are risks of declining usage and financial exclusion which are analysed below

1. Impact on Transaction Volume:

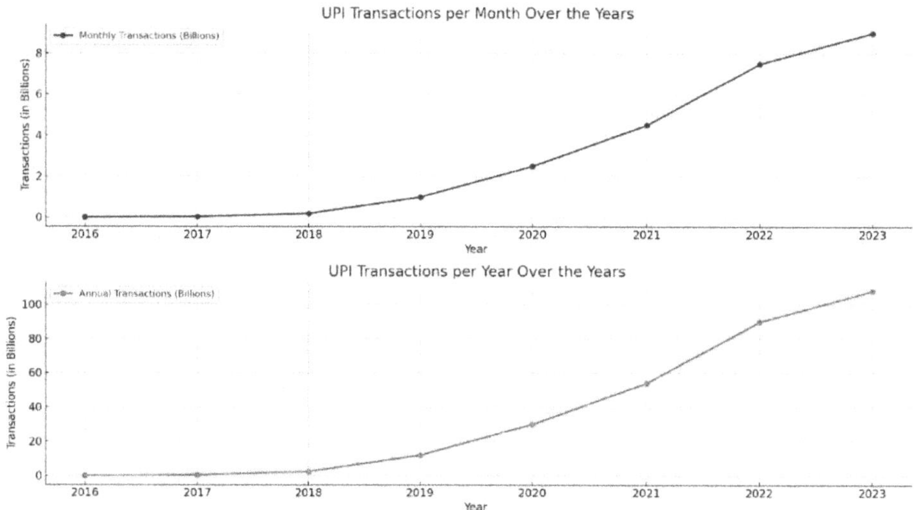

Decline in Microtransactions: UPI is widely used for small-value transactions (e.g., groceries, cab fares, etc.). A fee could discourage users from making frequent small payments and opting for alternative methods.

Shift to Other Payment Methods: Users may shift to cash, debit/credit cards, or alternative mobile wallets that do not impose a fee.

Impact on Digital Inclusion: UPI has greatly contributed to financial inclusion, especially among low-income users. Introducing fees could disproportionately affect these users and reduce their usage.

Merchant Impact: Small businesses that rely on UPI payments may also be affected, leading to a decline in overall digital payment adoption.

However, this could end differently also. Considering the **80-20 rule**, even if UPI fees reduce the **volume** of transactions, a smaller portion of high-value transactions (likely 20%) would still account for the majority of **transaction value**. This means the government could still generate significant revenue from the small percentage of users who make large payments frequently. While the number of low-value transactions might drop, the bulk of the revenue would come from the 20% of transactions that contribute the most in terms of monetary value, thus cushioning the economic impact.

2. Impact on UPI Popularity:

UPI's widespread adoption is largely due the ease it has provided to people and also its **zero-fee structure**. Introducing a fee might reduce its popularity, especially among users who were previously drawn to the cost-free nature of the service.

Hypothetical Scenarios:

Scenario 1: A Small Fee (₹1 per transaction) – Moderate impact on small-value transactions, but users may still use UPI for convenience.

Scenario 2: A Percentage-Based Fee (e.g., 0.5%) – Greater impact on large-value transactions, potentially leading to a decline in high-volume payments. Now, let's look at hypothetical graphs to visualize how levying a fee might impact transaction volumes and popularity.

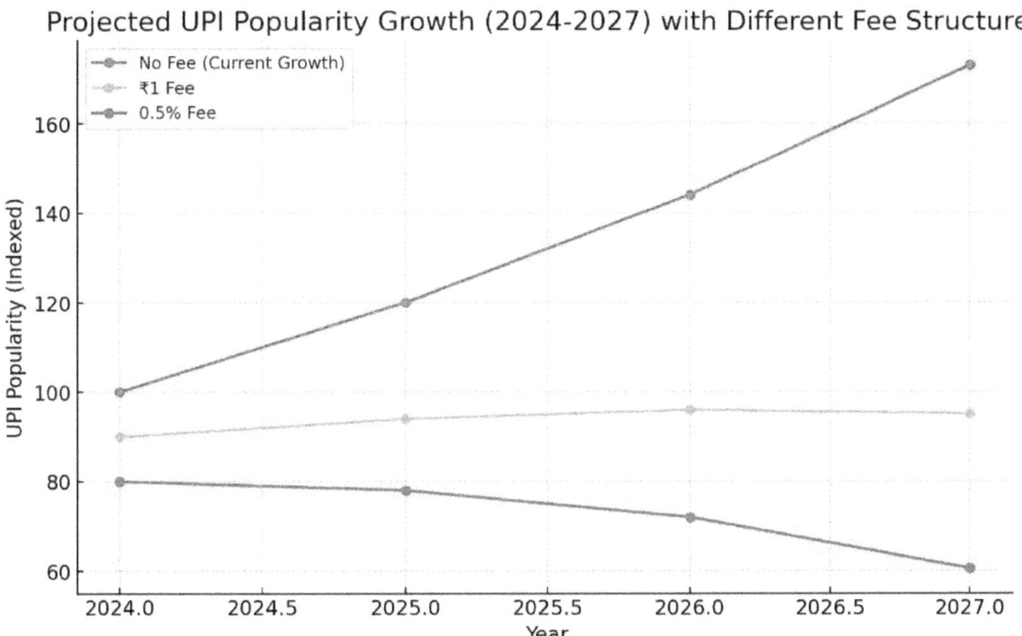

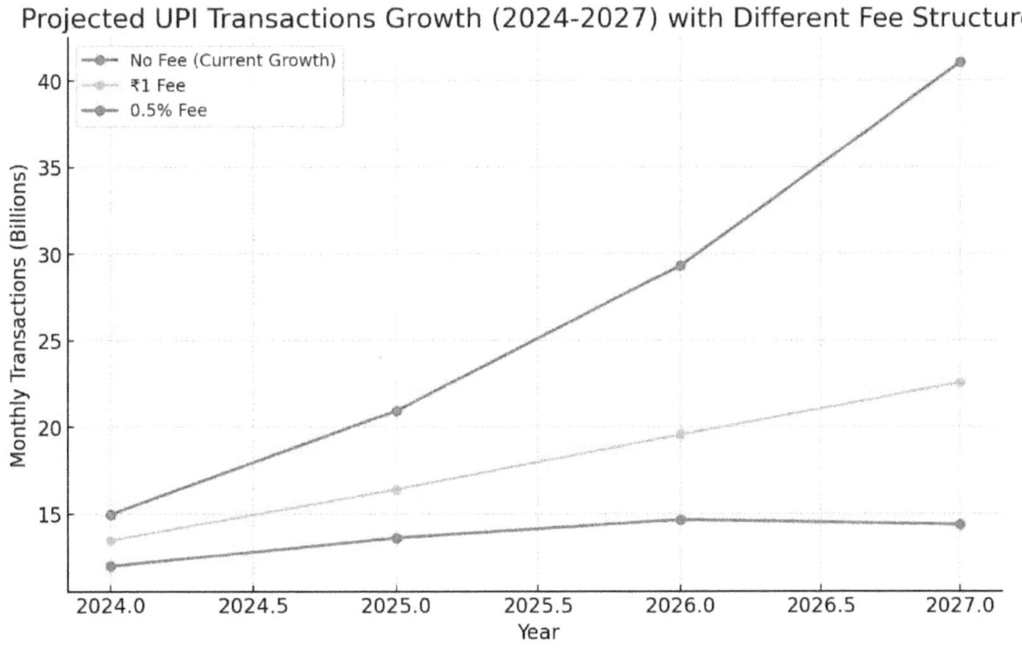

The Current growth rate of UPI in India is about 41% YoY growth compared to previous years (Based on data available on NPCI website). The projected decline in transactions is nil in the case of no fee, in the case of a 1-rupee fee a decline of about 45% is estimated (my estimate! I will explain how I estimated it.), in the case of 0.5% fee the estimated decrease in growth is about 65%.

While the initial decline may be higher, it is also possible that the people adapt to this fee and subsequently the decline would reduce in some years (or may even nullify altogether!!) and growth will follow up.

The question now arises, how did I estimate such huge numbers and why 45% and 65% only? The answer is that I took several factors and already existing data of surveys into consideration before coming up to these numbers. These are just my predictions, and the real numbers may or may not match my analysis as people may get used to the fee (if imposed) or some of them might even feel proud to pay a fee for the growth of nation! Who knows?

Getting back to the topic, below is an explanation of factors that I took into consideration-

1. ₹1 Fee Scenario (45% Decline)

The rationale behind estimating a **45% decline** by 2027 for a ₹1 fee is based on:

User Sensitivity: For microtransactions (which form a large portion of UPI payments), a flat ₹1 fee can feel disproportionately high. For instance, on a ₹100 transaction, a ₹1 fee represents a 1% cost, which could discourage users from using UPI for smaller payments. Users might switch to alternative methods (cash, cards) or reduce the frequency of payments.

Survey Data: A survey by the Economic Times in 2024 indicated that **70% of users would stop using UPI** if any fee were imposed (It is talked about this later in this article). However, I chose 45% as a conservative estimate to account for the fact that convenience and digital familiarity may still retain a portion of the user base, especially for higher-value transactions where ₹1 is relatively minor.

80-20 Rule Application: The assumption is that **20% of the users** who make high-value, less frequent transactions (and can absorb a ₹1 fee) will likely continue to use UPI. However, the **remaining 80%**, who use UPI primarily for microtransactions, could reduce their usage significantly. A decline of **45%** reflects this, where a moderate number of users shift back to cash or other payment methods due to the fee.

2. 0.5% Fee Scenario (65% Decline)

The **65% decline** under a 0.5% fee scenario is based on:

Higher Impact on Larger Transactions: A percentage-based fee affects larger transactions much more heavily than a flat fee. For instance, a 0.5% fee on a ₹10,000 transaction would result in a ₹50 charge, which could deter users making significant payments via UPI.

Fee Perception: Users making high-value payments, especially merchants handling large volumes, are likely to move away from UPI in favour of cheaper alternatives. A **65% decline** factors in the higher drop-off rate for large-value payments, which form a substantial portion of UPI's total transaction value.

Historical Behavior: Based on behavior in other payment ecosystems, percentage-based fees often lead to sharper declines in transaction volumes, as users avoid platforms with variable costs that increase with transaction size. The drop of **65%** reflects the likelihood that both micro and large transactions would reduce in significant numbers.

How the Decline Was Estimated

The 45% and 65% declines were estimated through the following approach:

Survey Data: The Economic Times survey indicated a high percentage of users would abandon UPI with any fee. This data was used as a foundation to estimate user behavior under fee scenarios.

Historical Patterns: Payment platforms that introduce fees tend to see a **sharp decline** in user engagement, particularly if free alternatives exist.

80-20 Rule: The assumption that 20% of high-value users account for the majority of the total transaction value, while 80% of low-value users form the bulk of the transaction count. A fee would disproportionately affect 80%, reducing overall volume.

Sensitivity to Fee Structure: The larger the fee (particularly percentage-based), the higher the decline due to the increased financial burden on users and merchants.

Thus, the **45% and 65% declines** represent a model of UPI's potential response to fees, combining behavioural patterns, historical analogies, and user feedback from surveys.

While the hypothetical graphs suggest decline in the transactions, A survey conducted by The Economic Times

THE ECONOMIC TIMES | Industry

English Edition ▾ | **Today's ePaper**

Subscribe   Sign In

Avail 15 Days Free Trial

☰ Home ETPrime Markets Market Data News Industry Rise Politics Wealth MF Tech Careers Opinion NRI Panache ET TV Spotlight ⋮

Auto ▾ Banking/Finance ▾ Cons. Products ▾ Energy ▾ Renewables ▾ Ind'l Goods/Svs ▾ Healthcare/Biotech ▾ Services ▾ Media/Entertainment ▾ More ▾

Business News › Industry › Banking/Finance › Finance › 70% users say will stop using UPI if fees levied

70% users say will stop using UPI if fees levied

ET Bureau · Last Updated: Mar 05, 2024, 12:17:00 AM IST

FOLLOW US SHARE FONT SIZE SAVE PRINT COMMENT

Synopsis

According to a survey by Local Circles, 7 out of 10 UPI users would stop using the app if transaction fees were imposed. Fintech companies have urged finance minister Nirmala Sitharaman to address the issue of implementing a merchant discount rate (MDR) in UPI transactions.

Most Searched Stocks

Indian Railway Finance   158.56
Corporation Share Price

in March 2024 revealed that a significant majority of users, approximately 70%, indicated they would stop using UPI if any transaction fees were imposed. This highlights the critical role UPI's fee-free structure plays in its widespread adoption, particularly for small-value transactions. The potential introduction of fees could drive users to explore alternative payment methods, posing a major challenge to the continued growth and success of the platform.

Link to study- 70% users say will stop using UPI if fees levied - The Economic Times (indiatimes.com)

Now we will talk about the popularity graphs, how it is calculated and other things related to it in detail-

1. What Does Popularity Represent?

Popularity here reflects the overall user acceptance, awareness, and willingness to use UPI. It's influenced by:

Number of Active Users: More users adopting UPI increases its popularity.

Transaction Volume: A higher number of transactions indicates that UPI is not only popular but widely used.

Convenience vs. Cost: As long as UPI remains free or minimally costly, users perceive it as a convenient and attractive option.

2. How Is Popularity Calculated?

Popularity was indexed to a base value of 100 in 2024, assuming that at the current growth trajectory, UPI's usage would naturally increase over the years without fees. Here's how it was calculated:

Base Popularity (No Fee): Starting from 100 in 2024, I projected a 20% annual growth rate in popularity based on UPI's increasing transaction volume and user base. The growth pattern followed the rise in the number of active users and transactions. By 2027, popularity reaches an index value of 173 if no fee is imposed.

₹1 Fee Scenario:

A flat fee could lead to dissatisfaction among users, particularly affecting low-value transactions. As discussed earlier, surveys suggest a large chunk of users would stop using UPI altogether if fees are introduced.

Assuming that 45% of transactions are lost, a similar 45% decline in popularity is expected by 2027, meaning popularity would drop to 95 (173 - 45%).

0.5% Fee Scenario:

A percentage-based fee could have a much stronger negative impact, especially on large-value transactions. Users who regularly transfer significant sums are more likely to abandon the platform, perceiving it as too costly.

With a 65% drop in transaction volume, I projected a 65% decline in popularity, resulting in a score of 61 by 2027.

3. Relation Between Popularity and Growth

Popularity and Transaction Growth: There is a direct correlation between popularity and transaction volume. The more popular a digital payment method is, the more users adopt it, and consequently, the more transactions occur. For UPI, this means that:

As transaction volume increases, popularity tends to rise due to positive word of mouth, ease of access, and improved financial inclusion.

Conversely, if transaction volume declines (due to fees or other factors), popularity declines as users migrate to other payment methods like cash or alternative digital wallets.

Popularity and Active Users: A significant part of UPI's popularity is driven by the number of active users. From 2024 to 2027:

If no fee is imposed, more users, including businesses and individuals, are expected to join the UPI ecosystem. This natural increase in the user base would lead to a 20-30% rise in popularity annually.

In the ₹1 fee scenario, we can expect a large chunk of the user base (45%) to shift away, especially those making smaller, frequent payments. As a result, the growth of new users would stall, and existing users would drop off, resulting in a decline in overall popularity.

In the 0.5% fee scenario, both large and small users would find UPI too expensive, and popularity would decline even more sharply.

Impact of Decline in UPI Transactions on Cash Usage

If UPI transactions were to decline significantly due to the introduction of fees, as suggested in the earlier hypothetical graphs, the country could see a shift back towards cash-based transactions. UPI has played a critical role in reducing cash dependency, especially for microtransactions and small businesses. A drop in UPI usage would lead to an increased reliance on cash, reversing some of the progress India has made toward becoming a less-cash-dependent economy.

If fees were selectively levied on UPI transactions above ₹1000 or on merchants/users making over 100 transactions per day, week, or month, the impact could be less severe.

Higher-Value Transactions: Charging a fee on transactions above ₹1000 could maintain the integrity of microtransactions while generating revenue from higher-value payments.

Street Vendors & Rural Users: Exempting small vendors and rural users would help protect financial inclusion while keeping UPI accessible to lower-income groups.

Urban Areas: Focusing fees on urban regions, where cash use is lower, could mitigate the decline in overall digital adoption.

Current Cash in Circulation and Required Cash with Decline in UPI

I will now provide a graph representing the current cash in circulation in the population and estimate how much more cash would be needed if UPI declines according to the earlier stated hypothetical scenarios.

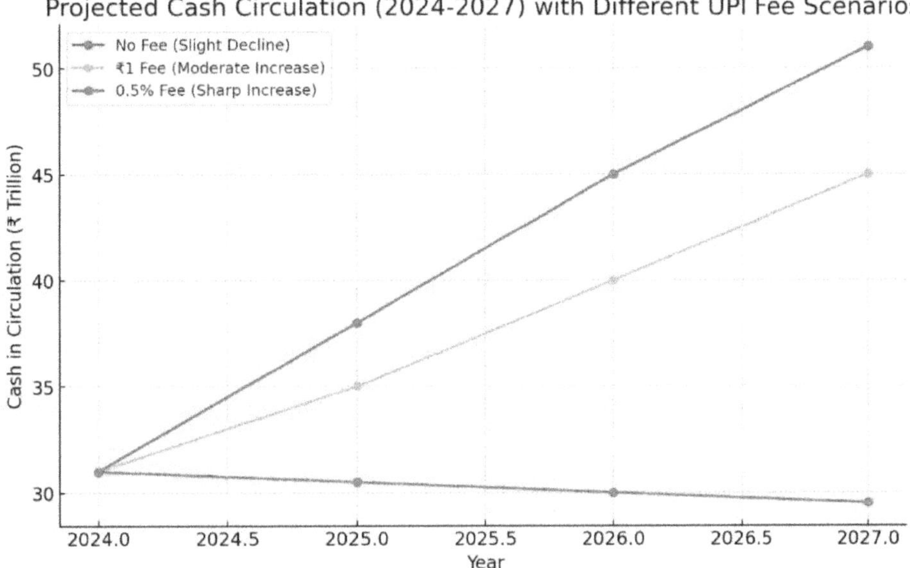

The graph above illustrates the potential impact of a decline in UPI transactions on cash circulation:

Impact on Cash Circulation:

No Fee: Slight decline in cash circulation as UPI use grows, reaching ₹29.5 trillion by 2027.

₹1 Fee: Cash circulation rises moderately to ₹45 trillion.

0.5% Fee: Cash circulation sharply increases to ₹51 trillion, reversing progress in digital payments.

This potential shift back to cash due to a decline in UPI transactions would not only increase demand for currency but also impose significant costs on the economy. Let us try to break down the details:

1. Cost of Producing Cash (Banknotes)

The **Reserve Bank of India (RBI)** bears the cost of producing currency notes. The cost of printing varies by denomination, but on average, it costs between **₹1.5 to ₹3** per banknote, depending on the security features and paper quality. For higher denominations, the cost tends to be on the higher end due to the added security features.

Denomination	Average Cost per Note (₹)
₹10	₹1.2 – ₹1.5
₹50	₹1.6 – ₹1.8
₹100	₹1.8 – ₹2.0
₹500	₹2.5 – ₹3.0

2. Cash Required Due to UPI Decline

Based on the earlier hypothetical scenarios:

In the **₹1 fee scenario (45% UPI decline)**, an additional **₹14 trillion** worth of cash would be required.

In the **0.5% fee scenario (65% UPI decline)**, an additional **₹20 trillion** would be needed.

Let us assume that the RBI distributes this increased cash demand across different denominations, particularly ₹100 and ₹500 notes, since these are the most used for daily transactions.

3. Cost of Printing Additional Cash

We can estimate the cost of producing this additional cash based on the proportion of currency distributed in different denominations. Let us assume a **60:40 distribution** between ₹500 and ₹100 notes, which is typical for the Indian currency system.

Cost Breakdown for the ₹1 Fee Scenario (45% decline, ₹14 trillion additional cash):

₹500 notes: ₹14 trillion × 60% = ₹8.4 trillion.

Required number of ₹500 notes = ₹8.4 trillion ÷ ₹500 = **16.8 billion notes**.

Cost of printing ₹500 notes = 16.8 billion × ₹3 = **₹50.4 billion**.

₹100 notes: ₹14 trillion × 40% = ₹5.6 trillion.

Required number of ₹100 notes = ₹5.6 trillion ÷ ₹100 = **56 billion notes**.

Cost of printing ₹100 notes = 56 billion × ₹2 = **₹112 billion**.

Total printing cost for ₹14 trillion = ₹50.4 billion + ₹112 billion = **₹162.4 billion** (₹16,240 crore).

Cost Breakdown for the 0.5% Fee Scenario (65% decline, ₹20 trillion additional cash):

₹500 notes: ₹20 trillion × 60% = ₹12 trillion.

Required number of ₹500 notes = ₹12 trillion ÷ ₹500 = **24 billion notes**.

Cost of printing ₹500 notes = 24 billion × ₹3 = **₹72 billion**.

₹100 notes: ₹20 trillion × 40% = ₹8 trillion.

Required number of ₹100 notes = ₹8 trillion ÷ ₹100 = **80 billion notes**.

Cost of printing ₹100 notes = 80 billion × ₹2 = **₹160 billion**.

Total printing cost for ₹20 trillion = ₹72 billion + ₹160 billion = **₹232 billion** (₹23,200 crore).

Summary of Costs:

₹1 Fee Scenario (45% decline): Printing an additional **₹14 trillion** in cash would cost around **₹162.4 billion** (₹16,240 crore).

0.5% Fee Scenario (65% decline): Printing an additional **₹20 trillion** in cash would cost around **₹232 billion** (₹23,200 crore).

In both cases, the additional costs would be a significant financial burden on the RBI and could potentially trickle down to consumers through banking fees or reduced government spending elsewhere. The operational and logistical challenges of handling a higher cash demand further complicate the situation, emphasizing the negative impact of discouraging UPI transactions.

The potential decline in UPI transactions due to the introduction of fees would not only affect end-users and businesses but also have significant ramifications for the third parties involved in the UPI ecosystem

To understand impact of Extra Expenditure on Indian economy let us discuss some of the key impacts in detail-

1. Currency Printing Cost

Impact: As the shift from digital to cash-based transactions occurs due to a decline in UPI usage, the demand for cash will rise significantly. This will lead to an increase in the cost of printing currency.

Data Breakdown: Based on earlier estimations, the cost of printing additional cash was calculated for both hypothetical fee scenarios:

In the ₹1 fee scenario (45% decline in UPI transactions), an additional ₹14 trillion would be needed in cash circulation. The cost of printing this additional currency was calculated to be approximately ₹16,240 crore.

In the 0.5% fee scenario (65% decline in UPI transactions), an additional ₹20 trillion would be required, with an estimated cost of ₹23,200 crore.

Source: The data on the cost of currency printing comes from the annual reports of the Reserve Bank of India (RBI), where it provides the cost per note for various denominations (₹3 per ₹500 note, ₹2 per ₹100 note). These figures are then applied to the required cash volumes.

2. Increased ATM Refills and Logistics

Impact: With a significant shift back to cash, ATMs will need to be refilled more frequently to meet the increased cash demand. This would raise logistical costs related to transporting, securing, and maintaining currency.

Data Breakdown: The exact cost increase varies but is estimated to grow by at least 20% in the ₹1 fee scenario due to a surge in cash demand, and by up to 35% in the 0.5% fee scenario. Increased cash handling not only imposes higher operational costs on banks but also affects security and transportation logistics.

Source: Information about ATM refilling costs and logistics comes from multiple banking sources, including reports from Cash Logistics Association of India and data from CMS Info Systems, a major cash management service in India.

For more details on this, you can visit: Cash Logistics Association Press Release(CMS Info Systems) and India Cash Vibrancy Report (CMS Info Systems).

3. Job Loss in the Digital Payment Sector

Impact: A significant decline in UPI transactions would result in job losses, particularly among the third parties that enable digital payments, such as payment aggregators, fintech companies, and customer service roles in digital payment providers.

Data Breakdown: The digital payments sector employs around 1.6 to 2.2 million people, including indirect jobs. A 45% decline in transaction volumes could result in the loss of 10-20% of jobs in this sector due to reduced revenues and reduced merchant transactions. In the 0.5% fee scenario, job losses could be as high as 25-30%. This implies the loss of hundreds of thousands of jobs, causing ripple effects on the broader economy.

Source: Employment data is compiled from various reports published by NASSCOM and other industry bodies like NPCI that track employment in fintech and digital payments.

4. Economic Growth Slowdown

Impact: The imposition of a fee on UPI transactions would not only affect microtransactions but also create a broader shift back toward cash. This would hinder financial inclusion efforts and slow down economic growth driven by digital payments.

Data Breakdown: In the ₹1 fee scenario, it is estimated that economic growth rate could slow down by approximately 0.2-0.3% per annum, while the 0.5% fee scenario could result in a more severe slowdown, with growth rate dropping by 0.5%. The underlying reason is that digital payments like UPI are pivotal for increasing the efficiency of economic transactions, reducing friction, and promoting transparency.

Source: These estimates are derived from projections by RBI and NITI Aayog on the economic impact of digital payments. Studies by McKinsey Global Institute also highlight the direct correlation between digital payment adoption and economic growth.

Digital India: Technology to transform a connected nation – A detailed analysis on how digital transformation can reshape India's economy (McKinsey & Company).

How digital finance could boost growth in emerging economies – This study explores the broader impacts of digital finance in emerging economies (McKinsey & Company).

These studies provide valuable insights into the economic impacts of digital payments, including the role of UPI in driving financial inclusion and growth.

However, based on the hypothetical impact of levying fees on UPI, we could expect the Indian economy to experience a reduction in **GDP growth rate** due to extra expenditure on printing cash, increased cash handling costs, and job losses. A decline of around **0.2% to 0.5%** in annual GDP growth could occur depending on the severity of UPI's decline.

This impact would slow down India's economic progress and reverse some gains made in the digital economy and financial inclusion, putting strain on the government's finances and increasing operational costs for businesses.

Conclusion:

Imposing a fee on UPI transactions presents both challenges and opportunities within India's digital payment ecosystem. While it may lead to an initial decline in transaction volumes as users explore alternatives like cash or other payment platforms, the long-term impact would largely depend on the approach taken by key stakeholders—government, financial institutions, and tech companies.

The resilience of UPI lies in its widespread adoption, ease of use, and government backing. Even in the face of transaction fees, UPI's integration into everyday financial activities—ranging from small-scale merchants to large businesses—suggests that users may adapt over time. Rather than a mass exodus to alternative payment methods, behavioural shifts may be more nuanced, with users adjusting to fees through selective usage for higher-value transactions while continuing to use UPI for its convenience and efficiency.

Moreover, introducing a fee could encourage innovation within the UPI ecosystem. Payment service providers, banks, and fintech companies might develop new incentive structures, such as loyalty programs, cash-back offers, or bundled services, to retain customers and enhance user experience. Similarly, the Government of India, recognizing the critical role UPI plays in driving financial inclusion, might implement a balanced approach—introducing tiered fees or subsidized models for lower-income groups to maintain UPI's accessibility for all.

Ultimately, the resilience of UPI will be tested by how well it can sustain its growth trajectory in the face of regulatory and economic changes. While hypothetical scenarios explore possible outcomes, the true impact of fees will only be revealed if such a policy is enacted. However, with UPI's deep integration into India's financial fabric, a well-considered and measured approach could ensure that it continues to thrive, offering secure, convenient, and inclusive digital payment solutions.

Guest Chapter 2: Lessons in Third-Party Risk Management from the Indus Valley Civilization

Author : *Mahesh Mohan Kanathezhath*

Experienced BCM and Resilience Management professional working for power and utility sector in Middle east.

In today's interconnected world, managing third-party risks is essential for maintaining the stability and security of business operations. Interestingly, the concept of third-party risk management is not new. It dates back to ancient civilizations, such as the Indus Valley Civilization (IVC), which thrived around 2500 BCE in the region that is now Pakistan and northwest India. This chapter delves into how the Indus Valley Civilization handled risks associated with external partnerships and the lessons contemporary businesses can learn from these practices.

The Indus Valley Civilization was one of the earliest urban societies, renowned for its sophisticated city planning, architecture, and social organization. Cities like Harappa and Mohenjo-Daro were characterized by grid layouts, advanced drainage systems, and significant public buildings. These cities were examples of meticulous urban planning, featuring standardized brick sizes and well-planned streets that facilitated efficient movement and communication. The civilization engaged in extensive trade with neighbouring regions, including Mesopotamia, indicating a complex network of third-party interactions. Trade artifacts such as seals and inscriptions found in Mesopotamia point to robust economic exchanges. The IVC's economy heavily relied on trade, both within the civilization and with distant lands. They traded goods such as cotton, metals, beads, and pottery. Managing these extensive trade networks required careful oversight to mitigate risks associated with external partners.

The IVC likely conducted thorough assessments of their trading partners, evaluating their reliability and trustworthiness. Artifacts suggest a standardized system of weights and measures, indicating efforts to ensure fairness and consistency in trade transactions. This level of standardization required a sophisticated understanding of quality control and risk management. Accurate documentation and record-keeping were essential for effective third-party risk management. Archaeological findings indicate that the IVC maintained meticulous records of trade transactions, possibly using seals and standardized scripts. This helped in tracking goods and ensuring accountability. These records also likely played a role in dispute resolution, providing evidence in cases of disagreements.

Key Aspect	Description
Urban Planning	Grid layouts, standardized brick sizes, advanced drainage systems, and significant public buildings
Trade	Extensive trade with Mesopotamia and other regions, involving goods such as cotton, metals, beads, and pottery
Standardization	Use of standardized weights and measures, standardized bricks
Documentation	Meticulous record-keeping using seals and standardized scripts
Legal Frameworks	Possible legal frameworks for managing trade disputes and enforcing agreements
Infrastructure	Robust transportation networks, including well-maintained roads and possibly riverine routes
Societal Structure	Emphasis on community collaboration and collective responsibility
Adaptability and Innovation	Centralized approach to construction and urban planning, adaptable based on local needs and resources

Key Aspects of the Indus Valley Civilization

Evidence suggests that the IVC had some form of legal frameworks to manage trade disputes and enforce agreements. While the specifics are not fully understood, the presence of uniform weights and measures hints at regulatory mechanisms. These frameworks would have been essential in maintaining order and trust in a complex trading system. Robust legal frameworks and well-defined contracts are crucial in managing third-party risks. These should clearly outline the roles, responsibilities, and expectations of all parties involved. The use of seals, for example, could have served as a form of contractual agreement, ensuring that both parties adhered to the terms of the trade.

The Indus Valley Civilization's advanced urban planning and infrastructure played a significant role in mitigating risks associated with third-party interactions. The uniformity in city layouts and building structures facilitated efficient management of resources and logistics. This standardization reduced the risks associated with construction and maintenance, ensuring stability in urban operations. The impressive drainage systems in cities like Mohenjo-Daro also highlight the importance of infrastructure in risk management, preventing flooding and ensuring sanitary conditions.

The IVC's economy heavily relied on trade, both within the civilization and with distant lands. They traded goods such as cotton, metals, beads, and pottery. Managing these extensive trade networks required careful oversight to mitigate risks associated with external partners. Below give a table on the best practice inspired from IVC practice.

Practice	Description
Partner Assessment	Evaluating trading partners' reliability and trustworthiness using standardized weights and measures
Documentation and Record-Keeping	Maintaining meticulous records of trade transactions to ensure accountability and assist in dispute resolution
Legal Frameworks	Implementing legal frameworks and well-defined contracts to manage trade disputes and enforce agreements
Standardization	Ensuring fairness and consistency in trade transactions through standardized weights, measures, and bricks
Infrastructure Investment	Developing advanced urban planning, drainage systems, and transportation networks to facilitate smooth movement of goods
Community Collaboration	Fostering a culture of trust and cooperation through collective efforts and resource sharing
Adaptability and Innovation	Adapting to changing circumstances and local needs through centralized but flexible urban planning and technology

Third-Party Risk Management Practices in IVC

The IVC developed extensive transportation networks, including well-maintained roads and possibly riverine routes. This facilitated the smooth movement of goods and reduced the risk of delays or losses in transit. Investing in robust logistics and transportation networks can significantly reduce third-party risks. These networks also allowed for the efficient mobilization of resources in times of need, showcasing an advanced understanding of logistics management.

The IVC's societal structure emphasized community collaboration and collective responsibility. This fostered a culture of trust and cooperation, which is essential for managing third-party relationships. Building a culture of collaboration and trust within an organization and with external partners can enhance third-party risk management. The presence of large public buildings and communal granaries indicates a society that valued collective efforts and resource sharing.

The IVC demonstrated adaptability and innovation in various aspects of their civilization, from urban planning to technology. This adaptability allowed them to respond effectively to changing circumstances and mitigate potential risks. For example, the use of standardized bricks across different cities suggests a centralized approach to construction and urban planning, which could be adapted based on local needs and resources.

The Indus Valley Civilization offers valuable lessons in third-party risk management that remain relevant today. By assessing partners carefully, maintaining thorough documentation, establishing robust legal frameworks, standardizing processes, investing in infrastructure, fostering collaboration, and embracing adaptability, modern businesses can effectively manage third-party risks. The ancient practices of the Indus Valley remind us that sound risk management principles are timeless and can be adapted to meet contemporary challenges. Modern organizations can draw inspiration from these ancient practices to build resilient and efficient systems for managing third-party risks.

Guest Chapter 3: An Old Case of Third-Party Risk Management

Author : Andrew Hiles

Founder - BCI, Professor Emeritus of BCM, Telfort business Institute, Shanghai University, Britanny, France.

Normally, Third Party Risk is that we may fail due to the failure of the third party. Typically, this could be a disruption in the supply chain caused by failure of a supplier for whatever reason.

In this most recent book, Damon Dev Sood has identified various types of third party risks.

However, there may be other situations of third party risks, like the example he includes of the recent CrowdStrike incident.

Here, the third party was ok, but it brought many companies to their knees through flawed software. Equally, TPRM needs to cover the possibility of impacts of actions by other stakeholders.

These include employees, by strikes, fraud, error, incompetence or sabotage.

One example is a small UK training company, MTS. A director stole its database and set up in opposition, causing MTS' bankruptcy. It is debatable whether this is entirely a case of third party risk, but the knew rival was certainly a third party. This third party risk emanated from insider risk (and Daman maintains that both go hand-in-hand).

Shareholders and other backers may cause massive adverse impact by withdrawing their support or, in the case of banks and insurers, miss-selling products.

A chronic example here is Clydesdale Bank, currently subject to two separate group actions, each for over £ 1 billion, each with over 2,000 plaintiffs.

A win for plaintiffs could lead to runs on its banks, contagion, disorderly markets, recession, and badly impact all past owners and its current owner, Nationwide. Anyone of these impacts could damage all Virgin Group companies, which seem to be propped up by opaque intra-Group and inter-Company loans.

Not only has Clydesdale Bank suffered record £ multi-million awards against it, twice, by the UK financial regulator, but top executives at Nationwide were warned as long ago as 2007 that its involvement in selling financial instruments linked to interest rate hedging products risked dragging it into a mis-selling scandal.

Defeat for the defendants in either of these group actions could lead to resurrection of all this bad news and cause a total collapse in public confidence in the whole UK banking system and its overseas activities, with possible contagion internationally in a world fragile with public debts exceeding GDP in many countries.

Companies that would be affected include Virgin's airlines and their supply chains from top to bottom, including Airbus, BAE, Rolls-Royce Engineering and all their suppliers and stakeholders.

This example is another angle of TPRM i.e. third parties, customers and stakeholders of a bank may fail due to the bank's failure.

There is yet another TPRM issue for UK companies.

That is the failure of duty of care by Companies House the registrar of UK companies, which those undertaking due diligence checks on the financial credibility of companies, trust to provide accurate information.

This trust was proved false by Clive Freedman QC, who established a duty of care against the Registrar of Companies in a high profile case. A company which had been in existence since 1900 was driven into administration within 7 weeks of a mistaken entry by the Registrar that the company was in liquidation. The mistake was to confuse a trading company Taylor & Sons Limited with another wholly unrelated company in liquidation, namely Taylor & Son Limited, and to enter the liquidation in the name of the wrong company. The former company, with the extra "s" in its name, was not in liquidation, but the effect of this publication was to affect the willingness of its customers and suppliers to continue to do business with it. In a trial of preliminary issues, Mr Justice Edis concluded that that there was no reason other than the mistaken entry for the Company going into administration.

Despite this, Companies House now still tries to hide behind its blanket waiver of duty of care and denies responsibility for the accuracy of its records, claiming it accepts and publishes information sent to it « in good faith ».

Thus, from 2003, after an open-ended, open-dated charge, known as a debenture, was placed on Kingswell International [ki] by Clydesdale Bank, in addition to the mortgage on the house that was security for the loan from the Bank.

Companies House published the debenture, wrongly showing it as unpaid, for some 15 years, despite the debenture having been fully repaid in July 2003.

Clydesdale Bank should have notified Companies House, in 2003, of the repayment of the mortgage and cancelled the debenture, but failed to do so until about 2017, when its existence was, for the first time, brought to the attention of the second KI director by an ethical competitor.

Even then, the Bank declined to close the debenture until, eventually, KI's accountant had the debenture marked as discharged by Companies House.

The debenture was proved to have been unjustified and unfair by the sale of the mortgaged house to the first viewer on the first day it was put on the market, for the full asking price.

The sale proceeds were immediately used to repay the outstanding part of the mortgage in full.

This long-running unfair situation defamed KI, its directors, and stifled KI's business, as prospects, credit agencies and existing clients discovered the debenture when they checked KI's financial credibility, a process known as 'due diligence'.

Sample TPRMF, Third Party Policy, and Third Party Strategy

I am happy to include these three assets which are very difficult to find. The inspiration to include these at the last moment came from BCBS Consultative Document <u>Principles for the sound management of third-party risk (bis.org)</u>.

Third Party Risk Management Framework

1. Introduction

The Third-Party Risk Management Framework (TPRMF) is a comprehensive approach designed to manage the risks associated with third-party service providers (TPSPs). It aligns with the organization's overall risk management framework and provides detailed guidelines for due diligence, risk assessment, monitoring, and governance of third-party relationships.

2. Objectives of TPRMF

The objectives of the TPRMF are to:

Ensure that third-party relationships support the organization's strategic and operational objectives.

Mitigate financial, operational, legal, and reputational risks posed by TPSPs.

Maintain operational resilience by ensuring critical third-party services are reliable and secure.

Ensure compliance with applicable regulations and industry standards.

3. Components of the TPRMF

Components at a glance:

Governance and Oversight: Clear roles and responsibilities, with board approval and ongoing oversight.

Risk Identification: Classifying TPSPs by the level of criticality and risk.

Risk Appetite: Defining risk tolerance for TPSP disruptions, integrating KRIs, and stress testing.

Due Diligence: Pre-contract assessment of financial stability, cybersecurity, compliance.

Contracts: SLAs, liability, audit clauses.

Monitoring: Continuous evaluation, real-time risk tracking.

Scenario Testing: Assess TPSP disruption impacts and inclusion in BC/DR plans.

Contingency Planning: Exit strategies and alternative vendor plans.

Training: Ongoing education on TPSP risks.

Reporting: Regular risk updates to senior management.

Review: Annual reassessment and updates.

Integration: Linking TPRMF to the overall risk management framework.

a) Governance and Oversight

Establish a clear governance structure with defined roles and responsibilities for managing third-party risks.

The board of directors and senior management must approve the TPRMF and oversee its implementation.

Establish a Third-Party Risk Management Committee to monitor ongoing third-party risks.

b) Third-Party Risk Identification and Categorization

Identify and categorize third-party service providers based on the criticality of the services they provide and the risks they pose to the organization.

Critical TPSPs are those that could significantly impact business continuity, data security, and regulatory compliance if they fail.

c) Risk Appetite and Tolerances

Define risk appetite and tolerance levels for third-party arrangements in alignment with the organization's overall risk management strategy.

Identify key risk indicators (KRIs) to measure and monitor third-party risk exposure.

Include disruption tolerances for critical third-party services and ensure they are forward-looking, incorporating scenario analysis and stress testing.

d) Due Diligence and Selection Criteria

Implement a robust due diligence process before onboarding any TPSP. This should assess financial stability, operational capabilities, data security posture, regulatory compliance, and overall risk management practices.

Third-party selection should also consider geopolitical risks, supply chain dependencies, and the potential for concentration risks.

e) Contractual Agreements and Risk Transfer

Ensure all third-party relationships are governed by formal contracts outlining service level agreements (SLAs), performance expectations, liability limitations, and provisions for risk-sharing.

Contracts should include clauses for ongoing audits, compliance assessments, and the right to terminate the relationship if risk thresholds are breached.

f) Ongoing Monitoring and Auditing

Continuously monitor TPSPs through performance reviews, audits, and compliance assessments to ensure they meet contractual obligations and performance standards.

Implement technology solutions for real-time monitoring of cybersecurity risks, operational disruptions, and vendor performance metrics.

Periodically reassess third-party risks based on evolving external factors, including new regulations, economic changes, or technological advancements.

g) Scenario Planning and Stress Testing

Conduct scenario analysis and stress testing to evaluate the potential impacts of TPSP disruptions on the organization's operations, financial performance, and customer service.

Include TPSPs in the organization's business continuity and disaster recovery plans, ensuring they have their own plans in place.

h)   Risk Mitigation and Contingency Planning

Develop contingency plans for key TPSPs, identifying alternative vendors and backup solutions for critical services.

Establish clear exit strategies in case the TPSP fails to meet performance expectations or introduces excessive risks to the organization.

i)   Training and Capacity Building

Provide regular training for employees involved in managing third-party relationships, ensuring they understand the risks and their responsibilities.

Develop expertise in managing emerging risks related to new technologies, geopolitical shifts, and supply chain vulnerabilities.

j)   Reporting and Communication

Establish a comprehensive reporting mechanism to regularly communicate third-party risk exposure to the board of directors and senior management.

Maintain an open line of communication with third-party service providers, ensuring transparency regarding any risks or issues that may arise.

k)   Review and Continual Improvement

The TPRMF will be reviewed annually to ensure it remains aligned with the organization's evolving business strategy, operational needs, and regulatory requirements.

The review process will incorporate lessons learned from prior third-party incidents, new industry standards, and emerging threats.

Updates to the framework will be presented to the board for approval, ensuring continued relevance and effectiveness.

l)   Integration with the Overall Risk Management Framework

The TPRMF must be fully integrated with the organization's broader risk management framework, ensuring that third-party risks are assessed and managed alongside other operational and strategic risks. This includes linking third-party risks to business continuity, operational resilience, and regulatory compliance processes.

Third Party Risk Management (TPRM) Policy

1. Introduction

This policy outlines the framework for managing risks associated with third-party relationships. It applies to all vendors, suppliers, contractors, consultants, and service providers that may affect the organization's operations, compliance, or reputation. The objective is to ensure that all third parties meet appropriate standards and that risks are identified, assessed, mitigated, and monitored consistently.

2. Scope

The TPRM Policy applies across the entire organization, including all departments and divisions engaging third parties. It covers:

Vendor Selection and Onboarding

Risk Assessments and Due Diligence

Contractual Safeguards

Ongoing Monitoring

Incident Response and Termination

3. Definitions

Third Party: Any external entity that provides goods, services, or technologies and has a business relationship with the organization.

Risk Assessment: A process of identifying, evaluating, and prioritizing risks posed by third parties.

Due Diligence: The investigation or audit of potential vendors to confirm all facts, including compliance, financial viability, security measures, and operational stability.

4. Governance

A cross-functional TPRM Committee will be responsible for overseeing third-party relationships and risk management. This committee will include representatives from legal, procurement, compliance, IT security, and risk management departments. The Committee will meet quarterly to review risk reports and vendor performance.

5. Vendor Segmentation

Vendors will be categorized based on criticality and risk exposure:

Critical Vendors: Those who have access to sensitive data or systems (e.g., IT providers, financial service vendors).

High-Risk Vendors: Those who could expose the company to significant regulatory, operational, or financial risks (e.g., healthcare suppliers, government contractors).

Low-Risk Vendors: Vendors providing non-critical goods or services (e.g., office supplies).

6. Risk Assessment and Due Diligence

Before onboarding, a comprehensive risk assessment must be conducted, including:

Financial Viability: To ensure the third party can fulfill long-term commitments.

Legal and Regulatory Compliance: To verify the third party complies with industry standards and relevant regulations.

Cybersecurity and Data Protection: For vendors handling sensitive data, a cybersecurity risk assessment is mandatory.

Operational Risks: Evaluate the third party's capacity to continue services under adverse conditions (business continuity and disaster recovery plans).

7. Contractual Safeguards

All third-party agreements should include clauses addressing:

Confidentiality and Data Security

Service Level Agreements (SLAs): To define the scope, quality, and timelines for deliverables.

Termination Rights: Include provisions for terminating the relationship due to breach of terms or unacceptable risk exposure.

Audit Rights: To allow the organization to conduct audits of the third party to ensure compliance.

8. Ongoing Monitoring

Third parties will be reviewed periodically on the risk tier they belong to:

Quarterly Reviews: For critical and high-risk vendors, including financial health checks and performance assessments.

Annual Reviews: For medium to low-risk vendors.

9. Incident Response

All third parties must have their own incident response plans, which should be integrated with the organization's incident management framework. In case of a breach, third parties must notify the organization immediately and cooperate in investigations and remedial actions.

10. Industry-Specific Considerations

Healthcare: Special focus on compliance with HIPAA (Health Insurance Portability and Accountability Act) to safeguard patient data. All third parties handling medical records must adhere to strict data privacy standards.

Pharmaceutical: Strict regulatory checks for compliance with FDA guidelines. Vendors involved in the supply chain for drug production must undergo rigorous audits to verify compliance with good manufacturing practices (GMP).

Utilities: Vendors providing essential services like electricity or water must be assessed for operational continuity, resilience, and compliance with regulatory bodies.

Telecom: Ensure third parties are compliant with cybersecurity frameworks such as NIST and that they protect customer data as per telecom-specific regulations.

Aviation: Focus on safety and compliance with international aviation regulations. Third parties involved in maintenance, repair, and operations (MRO) should be certified by relevant aviation authorities.

Government: Compliance with governmental procurement regulations and guidelines will be mandatory. Security clearances may be necessary for vendors handling sensitive government data.

Education: Vendors providing e-learning platforms or data management services must comply with privacy regulations.

Insurance: Third parties involved in claims processing and underwriting must adhere to insurance regulations.

Real Estate: Third parties involved in property management or leasing services should undergo checks for regulatory compliance (e.g., building codes and environmental regulations).

IT: Vendors providing cloud-based services or software must comply with industry standards for data protection, and ensure business continuity and disaster recovery plans are in place.

11. Training and Awareness

All employees involved in third-party management must undergo training on the TPRM Policy and procedures annually. Training will cover:

Vendor onboarding

Contract management

Risk assessment procedures

Incident management and response protocols

Offboarding

12. Reporting and Auditing

Quarterly reports on third-party risks and performance will be submitted to senior management. The internal audit team will perform an annual review of third-party relationships to ensure compliance with this policy and applicable regulations.

13. Policy Review

This TPRM Policy will be reviewed annually to ensure it remains relevant in light of emerging risks, regulatory changes, and industry standards.

A real TPRM policy can be found at assets.crawfordandcompany.com/media/2338714/global-third-party-risk-management-policy-oct-2017.pdf .

Third-Party Strategy

1. Introduction

This strategy provides a framework for managing third-party service provider (TPSP) relationships. It aligns with the organization's overall business strategy and risk management framework, ensuring that reliance on third-party services enhances operational efficiency while maintaining risk within acceptable limits. The strategy covers criteria for entering into, managing, and exiting from third-party arrangements.

2. Alignment with Business Strategy

The third-party strategy is designed to:

Support the organization's long-term business goals.

Enhance operational capabilities by leveraging external expertise and technology.

Ensure that reliance on TPSPs aligns with the organization's risk appetite and tolerance for disruption.

3. Criteria for Entering TPSP Arrangements

The strategy outlines specific factors to be considered before entering into third-party relationships, including:

Core vs. Non-Core Services: Evaluate whether a function is critical to the business and should remain in-house or can be safely outsourced to a third party. For example, key operational and data-intensive functions may require more stringent controls, whereas non-core functions (e.g., facilities management) may be easier to outsource.

Risk-Reward Analysis: Assess the risks, costs, and benefits of relying on a third party for specific services. This includes reviewing financial, operational, regulatory, and reputational impacts.

Vendor Selection: Conduct rigorous due diligence to ensure the third party meets performance, compliance, and risk management requirements.

4. Risk Evaluation and Ongoing Management

The organization will:

Continuously evaluate the risks associated with third-party relationships, considering factors such as cybersecurity risks, operational resilience, and regulatory compliance.

Ensure that third parties are subject to regular risk assessments, performance reviews, and audits to confirm ongoing suitability.

Implement stress testing and scenario analysis to understand the potential impacts of TPSP-related disruptions on critical business functions.

5. Exit Strategy

The strategy outlines clear exit conditions, including:

Performance Failure: Establishing that failure to meet predefined performance or compliance standards can trigger the exit from a TPSP arrangement.

Regulatory Breaches: Non-compliance with industry regulations or breach of legal agreements will also prompt termination of the relationship.

Operational Risk: If the third party introduces unacceptable levels of risk to the organization, contingency plans will be activated, and alternative providers will be engaged.

6. Disruption Tolerance

The organization's tolerance for operational disruption should consider the risks posed by third-party services. This includes:

Setting acceptable limits for disruptions to critical operations based on business continuity plans.

Including third-party risks in the organization's stress tests and scenario analysis to evaluate potential impacts.

Ensuring that third parties contribute to the organization's resilience by maintaining their own business continuity and disaster recovery plans.

7. Innovation and New Technologies

As part of this strategy, the organization will:

Evaluate the risks and benefits posed by adopting advanced technologies through third-party relationships, including the use of cloud services, artificial intelligence, and automation.

Ensure that all technological innovations align with the organization's risk appetite and contribute to long-term growth.

8. Training and Knowledge Management

The organization will maintain:

Adequate in-house knowledge and expertise to manage third-party relationships effectively.

Training programs to ensure that relevant employees understand the risks associated with third-party services and are able to manage these risks proactively.

Continuous learning initiatives to keep staff updated on evolving third-party risks and market trends.

9. Reporting and Oversight

Regular reporting of third-party risk exposure will be provided to the board of directors and senior management.

The organization will ensure that all third-party relationships are governed by contractual agreements that include clauses for monitoring, auditing, and exit.

10. Review and Update

This third-party strategy will be reviewed annually to ensure it remains aligned with the organization's evolving business strategy and external regulatory requirements. Any updates will be approved by the board of directors.

Case Studies in TPRM Implementation

These are fictitious case studies from 10 different industry sectors written with the intention of providing quick guidance for companies and professionals from those sectors to do the same and benefit in their Third Party Risk Management.

1. Financial Sector: United States

Introduction

The financial sector in the United States faces stringent regulatory requirements, with a strong focus on data security and compliance. Effective TPRM is crucial for financial institutions to manage third-party risks and ensure operational resilience.

Background

XYZ Bank, a leading financial institution in the U.S., decided to revamp its TPRM strategy following a series of incidents involving third-party vendors. These incidents highlighted significant gaps in their existing risk management framework. To address these challenges, XYZ Bank introduced a new role, the Chief Vendor Data Manager (CVDM), to oversee the management of vendor relationships and enhance the overall TPRM program.

The Challenge

Regulatory Compliance: Ensuring compliance with regulations such as GDPR, PCI-DSS, and SOX.

Data Security: Protecting sensitive customer data shared with third-party vendors.

Operational Risks: Managing disruptions caused by third-party failures or breaches.

Reputational Risks: Mitigating the impact of third-party incidents on the bank's reputation.

Vendor Due Diligence: Implementing robust due diligence processes to assess the risk profile of third-party vendors.

The Solution

Appointment of the CVDM: The CVDM led the vendor due diligence process, monitored vendor compliance, managed vendor data security, and coordinated incident response.

Enhanced Vendor Due Diligence: Detailed vendor assessments including background checks, financial health assessments, and security posture evaluations.

Risk Assessment and Categorization: Vendors were categorized based on their risk profile and criticality.

Contractual Safeguards: Vendor contracts included specific clauses related to data protection, regulatory compliance, incident reporting, and right to audit.

Continuous Monitoring: Continuous monitoring mechanisms to track vendor performance and compliance.

Incident Management: A robust incident management framework to address third-party incidents promptly.

The Outcome

Reduced Incidents: A 40% decrease in incidents involving third-party vendors.

Improved Compliance: Higher compliance levels with regulatory standards.

Enhanced Data Security: Fewer data breaches and better safeguarding of customer information.

Operational Resilience: Fewer disruptions in operations due to improved vendor performance.

Reputation Management: Proactive incident management helped mitigate the impact on the bank's reputation.

Conclusion

XYZ Bank's TPRM program, led by the CVDM, successfully mitigated third-party risks, ensuring regulatory compliance and operational resilience, ultimately enhancing customer trust.

The bank effectively used the following four newly developed tools:

i.   Third Party Due Diligence Cheat Sheet
ii.   Third Party Materiality Assessment Cheat Sheet
iii. Third Party Substitutivity Assessment Cheat Sheet
iv.   Third Party KPIs Evaluation Cheat Sheet

2. Healthcare Sector: United Kingdom

Introduction

The healthcare sector in the United Kingdom faces stringent regulations under the NHS and GDPR, requiring effective TPRM to manage risks related to patient data privacy, regulatory compliance, and service continuity.

Background

ABC Hospital, a leading healthcare provider in the UK, encountered several issues with its third-party vendors. To address these challenges, ABC Hospital introduced the role of a Chief Vendor Data Manager (CVDM) to oversee vendor relationship management and enhance their TPRM program.

The Challenge

Data Privacy: Ensuring patient data shared with third parties is protected in compliance with GDPR.

Regulatory Compliance: Adhering to NHS regulations and standards.

Service Continuity: Managing disruptions in medical supplies and services.

Vendor Performance: Ensuring that vendors meet quality and service standards.

The Solution

Appointment of the CVDM: The CVDM led the effort to enhance vendor due diligence, data security, and compliance monitoring.

Enhanced Vendor Due Diligence: Comprehensive assessments of vendor capabilities, compliance, and security measures.

Risk Categorization: Categorizing vendors based on their impact on patient care and data security.

Continuous Monitoring: Implementing real-time monitoring of vendor performance and compliance.

Incident Management: Establishing protocols for managing vendor-related incidents.

The Outcome

Improved Compliance: Higher adherence to GDPR and NHS regulations.

Enhanced Data Security: Fewer data breaches and better protection of patient information.

Better Service Continuity: Reduced disruptions in medical supplies and services.

Improved Vendor Performance: Enhanced quality and reliability of third-party services.

Conclusion

ABC Hospital's TPRM program, led by the CVDM, successfully mitigated third-party risks, ensuring regulatory compliance and service continuity, ultimately enhancing patient care.

The hospital effectively used the following four newly developed tools:

i. Third Party Due Diligence Cheat Sheet
ii. Third Party Materiality Assessment Cheat Sheet
iii. Third Party Substitutivity Assessment Cheat Sheet
iv. Third Party KPIs Evaluation Cheat Sheet

3. Pharmaceutical Sector: Germany

Introduction

The pharmaceutical sector in Germany faces stringent regulatory requirements under the European Medicines Agency (EMA) and GDPR, requiring effective TPRM to manage risks related to regulatory compliance, data security, and supply chain integrity.

Background

PharmaCo, a leading pharmaceutical company in Germany, faced significant challenges with third-party vendors. To tackle these issues, PharmaCo appointed a Chief Vendor Data Manager (CVDM) to enhance their TPRM strategy.

The Challenge

Regulatory Compliance: Ensuring vendors comply with EMA regulations and Good Manufacturing Practices (GMP).

Data Security: Protecting sensitive research data shared with vendors.

Supply Chain Integrity: Managing risks in the production and distribution of pharmaceuticals.

Quality Control: Ensuring vendors meet stringent quality standards.

The Solution

Appointment of the CVDM: The CVDM led initiatives to strengthen vendor assessments, compliance, and data security.

Enhanced Vendor Due Diligence: Rigorous evaluations of vendor compliance with EMA regulations and GMP through Due Diligence Tool.

Risk Categorization: Classifying vendors based on their criticality to the supply chain and data security through Materiality Assessment Tool.

Continuous Monitoring: Real-time tracking of vendor compliance and performance through KPIs Evaluation Tool.

Incident Management: Establishing protocols for managing vendor-related incidents.

The Outcome

Improved Compliance: Higher compliance rates with EMA regulations and GMP.

Enhanced Data Security: Reduced incidents of data breaches.

Better Supply Chain Integrity: Fewer disruptions in production and distribution.

Improved Quality Control: Enhanced product quality and safety.

Conclusion

PharmaCo's TPRM program, led by the CVDM, successfully addressed third-party risks, ensuring regulatory compliance and supply chain integrity, ultimately safeguarding public health.

The pharma company effectively used the following four newly developed tools:

i. Third Party Due Diligence Cheat Sheet
ii. Third Party Materiality Assessment Cheat Sheet
iii. Third Party Substitutivity Assessment Cheat Sheet
iv. Third Party KPIs Evaluation Cheat Sheet

4. Utilities Sector: Australia

Introduction

The utilities sector in Australia faces critical risks related to operational continuity, cybersecurity, and regulatory compliance under the Australian Energy Regulator (AER) and Privacy Act. Effective TPRM is essential to manage these risks.

Background

PowerGrid, a major utility provider in Australia, faced challenges with third-party vendors, including cybersecurity threats and operational disruptions. To mitigate these risks, PowerGrid introduced the role of a Chief Vendor Data Manager (CVDM) under a comprehensive and revamped Third Party Risk Management Program.

The Challenge

Operational Continuity: Ensuring uninterrupted service delivery.

Cybersecurity: Protecting critical infrastructure from cyber threats.

Regulatory Compliance: Adhering to AER regulations and the Privacy Act.

Vendor Performance: Maintaining high standards of service from third-party vendors.

The Solution

Appointment of the CVDM: The CVDM led efforts to enhance vendor assessments, cybersecurity measures, and compliance monitoring.

Enhanced Vendor Due Diligence: Comprehensive evaluations of vendor capabilities, security measures, and compliance through Due Diligence Tool.

Risk Categorization: Classifying vendors based on their impact on operational continuity and cybersecurity.

Continuous Monitoring: Real-time monitoring of vendor performance and security through KPIs Evaluation Tool.

Incident Management: Establishing protocols for managing vendor-related incidents.

The Outcome

Improved Continuity: Reduced operational disruptions.

Enhanced Cybersecurity: Fewer cyber incidents affecting critical infrastructure.

Better Compliance: Higher adherence to AER regulations and the Privacy Act.

Improved Vendor Performance: Enhanced reliability and service quality from vendors.

Conclusion

PowerGrid's TPRM program, led by the CVDM, effectively mitigated third-party risks, ensuring operational continuity and cybersecurity, ultimately safeguarding national infrastructure.

The utility company effectively used the following four newly developed tools:

i. Third Party Due Diligence Cheat Sheet
ii. Third Party Materiality Assessment Cheat Sheet
iii. Third Party Substitutivity Assessment Cheat Sheet
iv. Third Party KPIs Evaluation Cheat Sheet

5. Telecom Sector: India

Introduction

The telecom sector in India faces unique challenges related to data privacy, regulatory compliance, and service continuity under the Telecom Regulatory Authority of India (TRAI) and the IT Act. Effective Third-Party Risk Management (TPRM) is essential to manage these risks.

Background

TeleComCo, a leading telecom provider in India, proactively decided to make improvements in its TPRM program to provide better services to its customers. To this effect, they appointed a Chief Vendor Data Manager (CVDM).

The Challenge

1. Data Privacy: Protecting customer data shared with third parties in compliance with the IT Act.

2. Regulatory Compliance: Adhering to TRAI regulations and standards.

3. Service Continuity: Managing disruptions in network and customer services.

4. Vendor Performance: Ensuring vendors meet quality and service standards.

The Solution

1. Appointment of the CVDM: The CVDM led efforts to enhance vendor due diligence, data security, and compliance monitoring.

2. Enhanced Vendor Due Diligence: Rigorous assessments of vendor capabilities, compliance, and security measures through the Due Diligence Tool.

3. Risk Categorization: Classifying vendors based on their impact on data privacy, regulatory compliance, and service continuity.

4. Continuous Monitoring: Implementing real-time monitoring of vendor performance and compliance through the KPIs Evaluation Tool.

5. Incident Management: Establishing protocols for managing data breaches and service disruptions related to third-party vendors.

6. Reducing Solo Dependencies: Identifying and onboarding additional vendors to mitigate risks associated with dependency on single vendors using the Materiality Assessment and Substitutivity Assessment Tools.

The Outcome

1. Enhanced Data Privacy: Reduced instances of data breaches and improved compliance with the IT Act.

2. Regulatory Compliance: Better adherence to TRAI regulations and standards.

3. Service Continuity: Fewer disruptions in network and customer services.

4. Improved Vendor Performance: Higher quality and reliability of third-party services and reduced solo dependencies.

Conclusion

TeleComCo's TPRM program, under the leadership of the CVDM, effectively managed third-party risks, ensuring data privacy, regulatory compliance, and service continuity, ultimately enhancing customer trust and satisfaction.

The telecom company effectively used the following four newly developed tools:

   i.   Third Party Due Diligence Cheat Sheet
  ii.   Third Party Materiality Assessment Cheat Sheet
 iii.   Third Party Substitutivity Assessment Cheat Sheet

iv.   Third Party KPIs Evaluation Cheat Sheet

6. Aviation Sector: Japan

Introduction

The aviation sector in Japan must manage complex risks related to safety, regulatory compliance, and operational continuity under the Civil Aviation Bureau (CAB) and data protection laws. Effective TPRM is crucial to address these challenges.

Background

SkyAir, a major airline in Japan, encountered difficulties with third-party vendors, including maintenance and service providers. To enhance its TPRM strategy, SkyAir introduced the role of Chief Vendor Data Manager (CVDM). Their main challenge was dependency on some solo third parties.

The Challenge

Safety Compliance: Ensuring vendors comply with safety regulations and standards set by the CAB.

Data Protection: Safeguarding passenger and operational data shared with third parties.

Operational Continuity: Managing risks related to disruptions in services and maintenance.

Vendor Performance: Ensuring that third-party service providers meet high standards of quality and finding a solution for solo dependencies.

The Solution

Appointment of the CVDM: The CVDM led efforts to improve vendor assessments, safety compliance, and data protection.

Enhanced Vendor Due Diligence: Detailed evaluations of vendor compliance with safety regulations and quality standards through Due Diligence Tool.

Risk Categorization: Classifying vendors based on their criticality to safety and operational continuity.

Continuous Monitoring: Real-time monitoring of vendor performance and safety compliance through KPIs Evaluation Tool.

Incident Management: Developing protocols for managing incidents related to third-party vendors.

Reducing Solo Dependencies: Identifying and onboarding new third parties through Materiality Assessment and Substitutivity Assessment Tools.

The Outcome

Improved Safety: Fewer incidents related to safety and maintenance.

Enhanced Data Protection: Reduced data breaches involving passenger information.

Operational Resilience: Fewer service disruptions and improved reliability.

Better Vendor Performance: Enhanced quality and reliability of third-party services and reduced solo dependencies.

Conclusion

SkyAir's TPRM program, guided by the CVDM, effectively managed third-party risks, ensuring safety compliance and operational resilience, ultimately enhancing passenger confidence and satisfaction.

The airline effectively used the following four newly developed tools:

v.   Third Party Due Diligence Cheat Sheet
vi.   Third Party Materiality Assessment Cheat Sheet
vii.   Third Party Substitutivity Assessment Cheat Sheet
viii.   Third Party KPIs Evaluation Cheat Sheet

7. Government Sector: Brazil

Introduction

The Brazilian government sector must navigate risks related to public service delivery, regulatory compliance, and data protection under laws such as the General Data Protection Law (LGPD). Effective TPRM is essential for managing these risks.

Background

GovBrazil, a large government agency in Brazil, faced challenges with third-party vendors, including issues with service delivery and data protection. To address these challenges, GovBrazil appointed a Chief Vendor Data Manager (CVDM).

The Challenge

Service Delivery: Ensuring reliable and effective delivery of public services by third parties.

Data Protection: Protecting sensitive data in compliance with the LGPD.

Regulatory Compliance: Adhering to Brazilian government regulations and standards.

Vendor Performance: Monitoring and managing vendor performance.

The Solution

Appointment of the CVDM: The CVDM led initiatives to enhance vendor assessments, data protection, and compliance monitoring.

Enhanced Vendor Due Diligence: Comprehensive evaluations of vendor capabilities, compliance with LGPD, and service delivery standards through Due Diligence Tool.

Risk Categorization: Classifying vendors based on their impact on public services and data protection.

Continuous Monitoring: Implementing real-time monitoring of vendor performance and compliance through KIPs Evaluation Tool.

Incident Management: Developing protocols for managing incidents involving third-party vendors.

The Outcome

Improved Service Delivery: Enhanced reliability and effectiveness of public services.

Better Data Protection: Fewer data breaches and better compliance with LGPD.

Higher Compliance: Improved adherence to government regulations.

Enhanced Vendor Performance: Improved quality and reliability of third-party services.

Conclusion

GovBrazil's TPRM program, led by the CVDM, successfully addressed third-party risks, ensuring better service delivery and data protection, ultimately enhancing public trust in government services.

The government agency effectively used the following four newly developed tools:

i.	Third Party Due Diligence Cheat Sheet
ii.	Third Party Materiality Assessment Cheat Sheet
iii.	Third Party Substitutivity Assessment Cheat Sheet
iv.	Third Party KPIs Evaluation Cheat Sheet

8. Education Sector: South Africa

Introduction

In South Africa, the education sector must manage risks related to data privacy, service continuity, and regulatory compliance under the Protection of Personal Information Act (POPIA). Effective TPRM is crucial for addressing these challenges.

Background

EduSouth, a prominent educational institution in South Africa, faced issues with third-party vendors affecting student data and service delivery. To enhance its TPRM strategy, EduSouth introduced the role of Chief Vendor Data Manager (CVDM).

The Challenge

Data Privacy: Protecting student and staff data in compliance with POPIA.

Service Continuity: Ensuring uninterrupted delivery of educational services.

Regulatory Compliance: Adhering to South African education regulations.

Vendor Performance: Managing and evaluating vendor performance.

The Solution

Appointment of the CVDM: The CVDM led efforts to strengthen vendor due diligence, data privacy measures, and compliance monitoring.

Enhanced Vendor Due Diligence: Thorough evaluations of vendor compliance with POPIA and service standards through Due Diligence Tool.

Risk Categorization: Classifying vendors based on their impact on data privacy and service delivery.

Continuous Monitoring: Implementing real-time monitoring of vendor performance and compliance through KPIs Evaluation Tool.

Incident Management: Establishing protocols for managing vendor-related incidents.

The Outcome

Enhanced Data Privacy: Fewer breaches of student and staff data.

Improved Service Continuity: Reduced disruptions in educational services.

Better Compliance: Higher adherence to POPIA and education regulations.

Improved Vendor Performance: Enhanced quality and reliability of third-party services.

Conclusion

EduSouth's TPRM program, led by the CVDM, effectively mitigated third-party risks, ensuring data privacy and service continuity, ultimately enhancing the educational experience.

The agency effectively used the following four newly developed tools:

   i.   Third Party Due Diligence Cheat Sheet
  ii.   Third Party Materiality Assessment Cheat Sheet
 iii.   Third Party Substitutivity Assessment Cheat Sheet
 iv.   Third Party KPIs Evaluation Cheat Sheet

9. Insurance Sector: Canada

Introduction

The insurance sector in Canada must manage risks related to data privacy, regulatory compliance, and service quality under the Personal Information Protection and Electronic Documents Act (PIPEDA) and industry standards. Effective TPRM is essential.

Background

InsureCan, a major insurance company in Canada, faced challenges with third-party vendors impacting data privacy and service delivery. To address these issues, InsureCan appointed a Chief Vendor Data Manager (CVDM).

The Challenge

Data Privacy: Protecting client information in compliance with PIPEDA.

Regulatory Compliance: Adhering to Canadian insurance regulations and standards.

Service Quality: Managing disruptions in claims processing and customer support.

Vendor Performance: Ensuring vendors meet quality standards.

The Solution

Appointment of the CVDM: The CVDM led initiatives to enhance vendor due diligence, data privacy measures, and compliance monitoring.

Enhanced Vendor Due Diligence: Rigorous evaluations of vendor compliance with PIPEDA and industry standards through Due Diligence Tool.

Risk Categorization: Classifying vendors based on their impact on data privacy and service quality.

Continuous Monitoring: Implementing real-time monitoring of vendor performance and compliance through KPIs Evaluation Tool.

Incident Management: Developing protocols for managing vendor-related incidents.

The Outcome

Improved Data Privacy: Fewer incidents of data breaches.

Better Compliance: Higher adherence to PIPEDA and insurance regulations.

Enhanced Service Quality: Fewer disruptions in claims processing and customer support.

Improved Vendor Performance: Enhanced reliability and service quality.

Conclusion

InsureCan's TPRM program, led by the CVDM, successfully managed third-party risks, ensuring data privacy and service quality, ultimately enhancing customer satisfaction.

The insurance company effectively used the following four newly developed tools:

   i.   Third Party Due Diligence Cheat Sheet
  ii.   Third Party Materiality Assessment Cheat Sheet
 iii.   Third Party Substitutivity Assessment Cheat Sheet
 iv.   Third Party KPIs Evaluation Cheat Sheet

10. Real Estate Sector: Mexico

Introduction

The real estate sector in Mexico must manage risks related to regulatory compliance, project management, and data security under local regulations and industry standards. Effective TPRM is crucial.

Background

RealEstateMX, a major real estate firm in Mexico, faced challenges with third-party vendors affecting project management and regulatory compliance. To address these issues, RealEstateMX introduced the role of Chief Vendor Data Manager (CVDM).

The Challenge

Regulatory Compliance: Ensuring compliance with Mexican real estate regulations and industry standards.

Data Security: Protecting sensitive data related to property transactions.

Project Management: Managing risks associated with construction and property management.

Vendor Performance: Ensuring vendors meet project deadlines and quality standards.

The Solution

Appointment of the CVDM: The CVDM led efforts to strengthen vendor assessments, data security, and compliance monitoring.

Enhanced Vendor Due Diligence: Thorough evaluations of vendor compliance with regulations and project management capabilities through Due Diligence Tool.

Risk Categorization: Classifying vendors based on their impact on project management and data security.

Continuous Monitoring: Real-time monitoring of vendor performance and compliance through KPIs Evaluation Tool.

Incident Management: Establishing protocols for managing project delays and data breaches.

The Outcome

Improved Compliance: Higher adherence to Mexican real estate regulations.

Enhanced Data Security: Reduced incidents of data breaches.

Better Project Management: Fewer project delays and improved property management.

Improved Vendor Performance: Enhanced quality and reliability of third-party services.

Conclusion

RealEstateMX's TPRM program, guided by the CVDM, effectively managed third-party risks, ensuring regulatory compliance and project success, ultimately enhancing client satisfaction.

The real estate company effectively used the following four newly developed tools:

i. Third Party Due Diligence Cheat Sheet
ii. Third Party Materiality Assessment Cheat Sheet
iii. Third Party Substitutivity Assessment Cheat Sheet
iv. Third Party KPIs Evaluation Cheat Sheet

Reader's views on various chapters

What is next for me?

The following writing projects are on:

1. 50+ Edible Projects for Families (part II)

2. Resiliency Testing

I hope that at least one will be picked up in 2025. The call for contributions (guest chapters) is open. Please write to me if you would like to avail this offer. I do not charge any fee for this.

Daman Dev Sood

Director – DBD Training & Consultancy (OPC) Private Limited

International Resilience Trainer & Consultant

FBCI, FBCS, CBCI, SMIEEE, M.IOD, ISO 22301 LA & Expert

Certified in Cybersecurity (ISC2)

IEEE Ambassador

Past Chair – IEEE Computer Society Delhi Section Chapter

Chair – PR&P Standing Committee, IEEE Delhi Section

Member Champion – IEEE India MOVE Partner Relations Committee

IEEE Computer Society Distinguished Contributor (Inaugural Class)

Toastmaster

Reskube Partner

Global Release - Global Emotional Impact Assessment Report – <u>click here to download complimentary copy</u>

Video profile: https://youtu.be/TuPmBmYDIms

Email: daman@damandevsood.com

Phone: +91 9958091880 (whatsapp)

https://medium.com/@damandevsood

https://in.pinterest.com/damandevsood

My Courses

S. No.	Course	Duration	Standard/ Area	Type
1	Certified Resiliency Testing Specialist **(CPD Certified)**	3 days	Resiliency	Instructor Led Online/ Classroom
2	Certified Organisational Resilience Professional	1 day	ISO 22316:2017	Instructor Led Online/ Classroom
3	Certified Organisational Resilience Specialist	3 days	ISO 22316:2017	Instructor Led Online/ Classroom
4	Certified Risk Management Professional	1 day	ISO 31000:2018	Instructor Led Online/ Classroom
5	Certified Risk Management Specialist	3 days	ISO 31000:2018	Instructor Led Online/ Classroom
6	Practical BIA (Specialist level)	2 days	BCM	Instructor Led Online/ Classroom

S. No.	Course	Duration	Standard/ Area	Type
7	Operational Resilience Foundation	½ day	Operational Resilience	Instructor Led Online/ Classroom
8	Certified Operational Resilience Professional	1 day	Operational Resilience	Instructor Led Online/ Classroom
9	Design, Develop, and Deliver an Effective BCM Test	2 days	BCM	Instructor Led Online/ Classroom
10	Daman's Thermometer	1 day	Crisis Communication	Instructor Led Online/ Classroom
11	Possibility Thinking	1 day	Softskills	Instructor Led Online/ Classroom

S. No.	Course	Duration	Standard/ Area	Type
12	Team Work & Art of Handling Questions	1 day	Softskills	Instructor Led Online/ Classroom
13	Resiliency Testing (for top management)	2 days	Resiliency	Instructor Led Online/ Classroom
14	Cyber Resiliency Testing (for top management)	1 day	Resiliency	Instructor Led Online/ Classroom
15	Certified Delivering Excellence Specialist **(CPD Certified)**	3 days	Resiliency	Instructor Led Online/ Classroom
16	Circular Economy, Life Cycle Analysis, ESG, and Sustainable Supply Chain	1 day	Sustainability	Instructor Led Online/ Classroom

Courses on Udemy

Delivering Excellence
In Management Consultancy and Program Management
Daman Sood
6.5 total hours · 44 lectures · All Levels
New

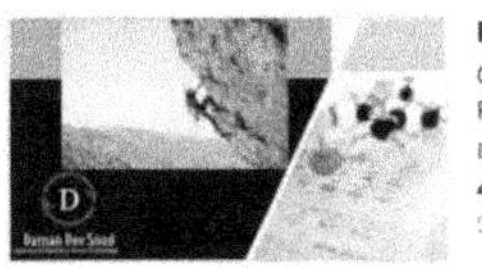

Fundamentals of Operational Resilience
Get Ready to be RIPER (Redeployable, Incrementable, Promotable, Employable, Retainable)
Daman Sood
4.4 ★★★★☆ (4)
2.5 total hours · 22 lectures · Beginner

Project Economics Essentials
Start delivering excellence to your customers by managing the economics of your projects and programs.
Daman Sood
1 total hour · 8 lectures · Intermediate

- https://www.udemy.com/course/delivering-excellence-managementconsultancy-customerdelight/
- https://www.udemy.com/course/fundamentals-of-operational-resilience/
- https://www.udemy.com/course/project-economics-essentials/

Copyrights Status

Course	Copyright Status
Organisational Resilience Specialist	Achieved
Organisational Resilience Professional	Achieved
Risk Management Professional	Achieved
Daman's thermometer	Achieved
Possibility Thinking	Achieved
Design, Develop, and Deliver an Effective BCM Test	Achieved
Practical BIA Course	Achieved
Teamwork and Art of Handling Questions	Achieved
Risk Management Specialist	Achieved
Operational Resilience Professional	Achieved
Resiliency Testing Specialist	Achieved
Delivering Excellence Specialist	Achieved

CERTIFICATE

OF

MEMBERSHIP

The CPD Certification Service
certifies that

Daman Dev Sood

is a MEMBER of
The CPD Certification Service

**Providing recognised independent CPD
accreditation compatible with global CPD
principles.**

Membership Number

17743

An initiative to increase standards of CPD
provision to professionals in relevant market
sectors

Date of Commencement: 9th June 2023

Authorised Signature: *G. Savage*

Managing Director, The CPD Certification Service

The Coach House, Ealing Green, London W5 5ER
Email: info@cpduk.co.uk Web: www.cpduk.co.uk
Tel: 020 8840 4383

The content of the following has been certified by
The CPD Certification Service as conforming to
Continuing Professional Development principles

**|Certified Delivering Excellence Specialist Course
Training Course**

MEMBER

**DAMAN DEV SOOD
(017743)**

Date:
July 2023

Certificate No:
47943

The Coach House, Ealing Green, London W5 5ER
E-mail: info@cpduk.co.uk   Web: www.cpduk.co.uk
Tel: 020 8840 4383

CPD
MEMBER
The CPD Certification
Service

CPD
CERTIFIED
The CPD Certification
Service

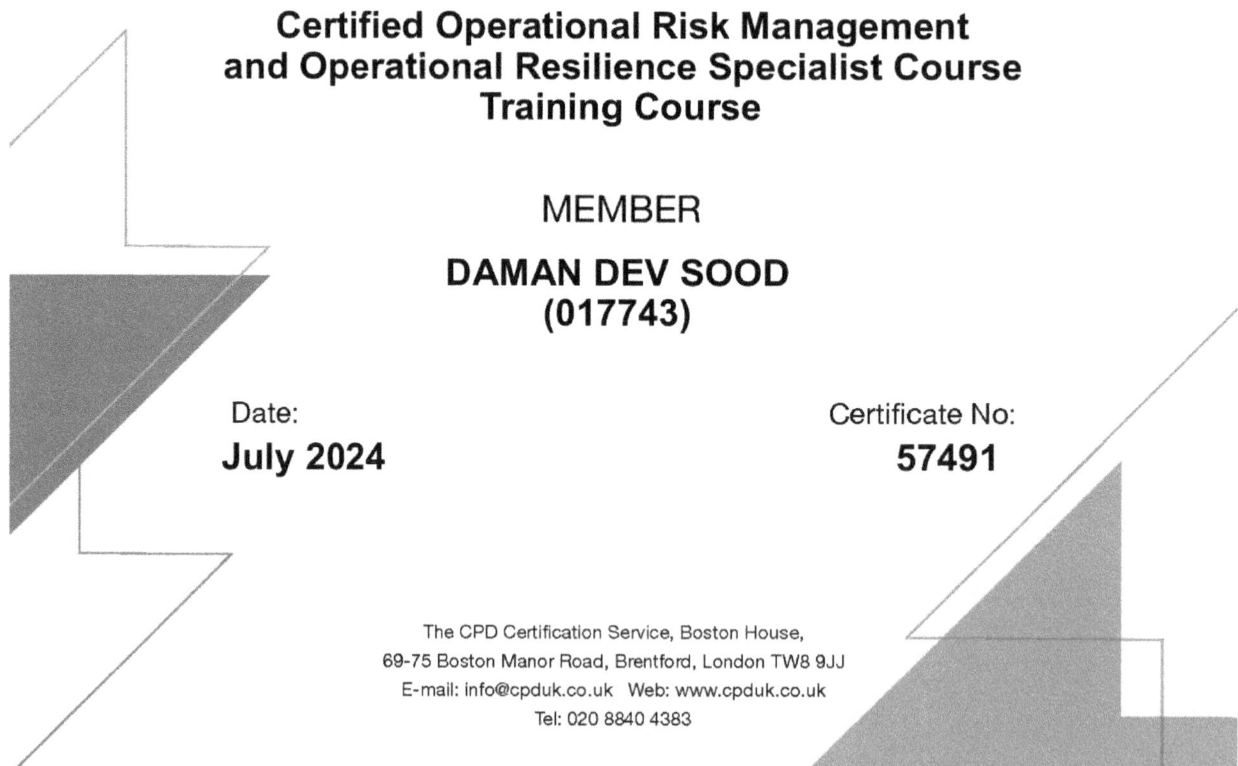
The content of the following has been certified by
The CPD Certification Service as conforming to
Continuing Professional Development principles

Certified Operational Risk Management
and Operational Resilience Specialist Course
Training Course

MEMBER

DAMAN DEV SOOD
(017743)

Date:
July 2024

Certificate No:
57491

The CPD Certification Service, Boston House,
69-75 Boston Manor Road, Brentford, London TW8 9JJ
E-mail: info@cpduk.co.uk   Web: www.cpduk.co.uk
Tel: 020 8840 4383

Other Books

BUSINESS
CONTINUITY
Implement BCM the UAE Way!
1st EDITION
STEP-BY-STEP GUIDE
AE/SCNS/NCEMA 7000:2015
TOWARDS NATIONAL RESILIENCE
Authors
DHIRAJ LAL
DAMAN DEV SOOD

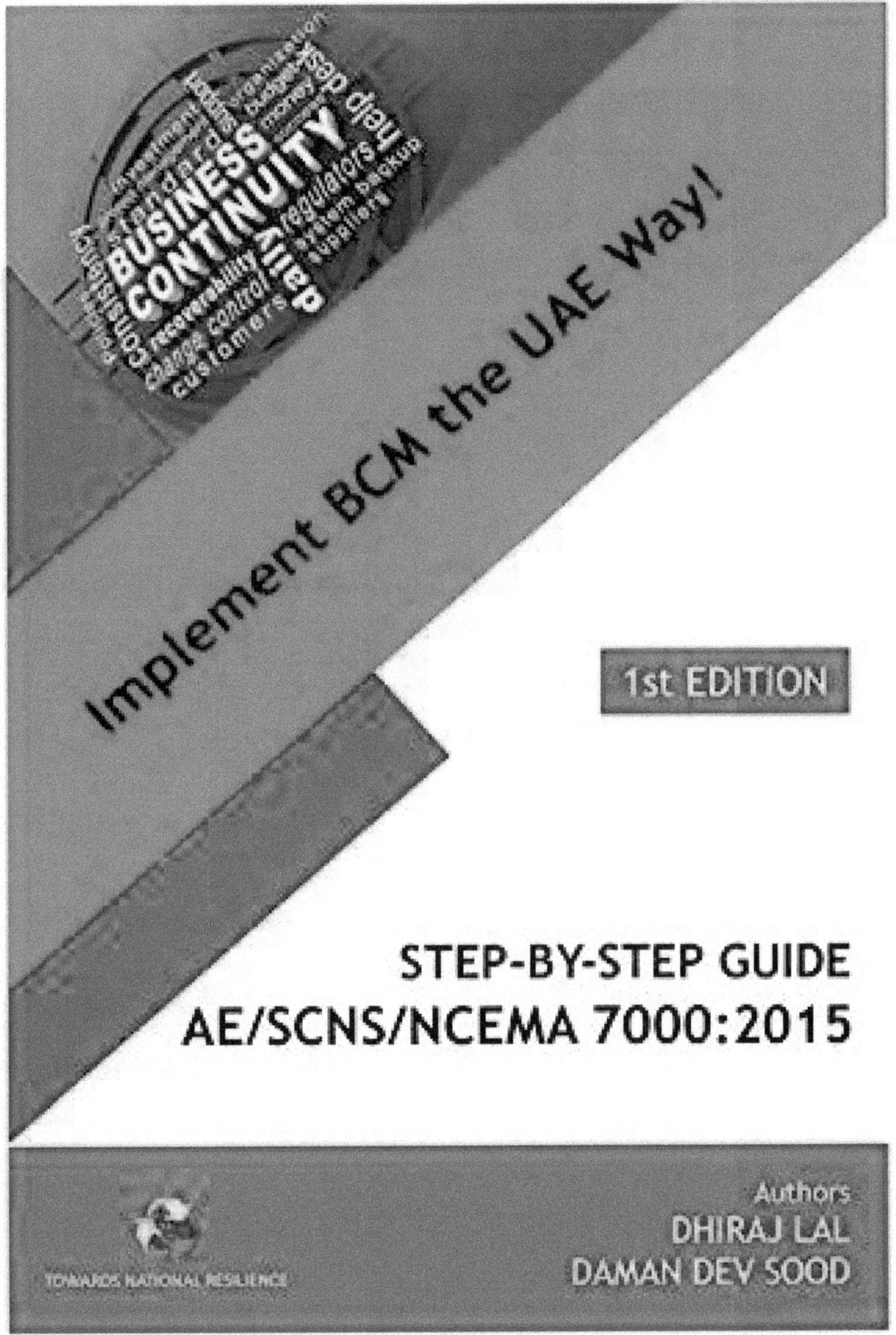

MY
EXPERIMENTS WITH
TRUTH BCM
MY BCM JOURNEY - YOUR BCM MENTOR/COMPANION
SUPPLY CHAIN CONTINUITY
DEPENDENCIES
BUDGET
IMPACT ANALYSIS
REVIEWS
RISK ASSESSMENT
INTERESTED PARTIES
CONTINUAL IMPROVEMENT
BUSINESS CONTINUITY MANAGEMENT
PLAN TESTING
CONTINUITY STRATEGIES
COMPETENCIES
REGULATORY REQUIREMENTS
CONTINUITY PLANS
IT DISASTER RECOVERY
DAMAN DEV SOOD

COPYRIGHT
Cases
Resolved
ALL RIGHTS RESERVED
COPYRIGHT
ALL RIGHTS RESERVED
ANCHITA SOOD
DAMAN DEV SOOD
cover designed by- Tanuj Sood

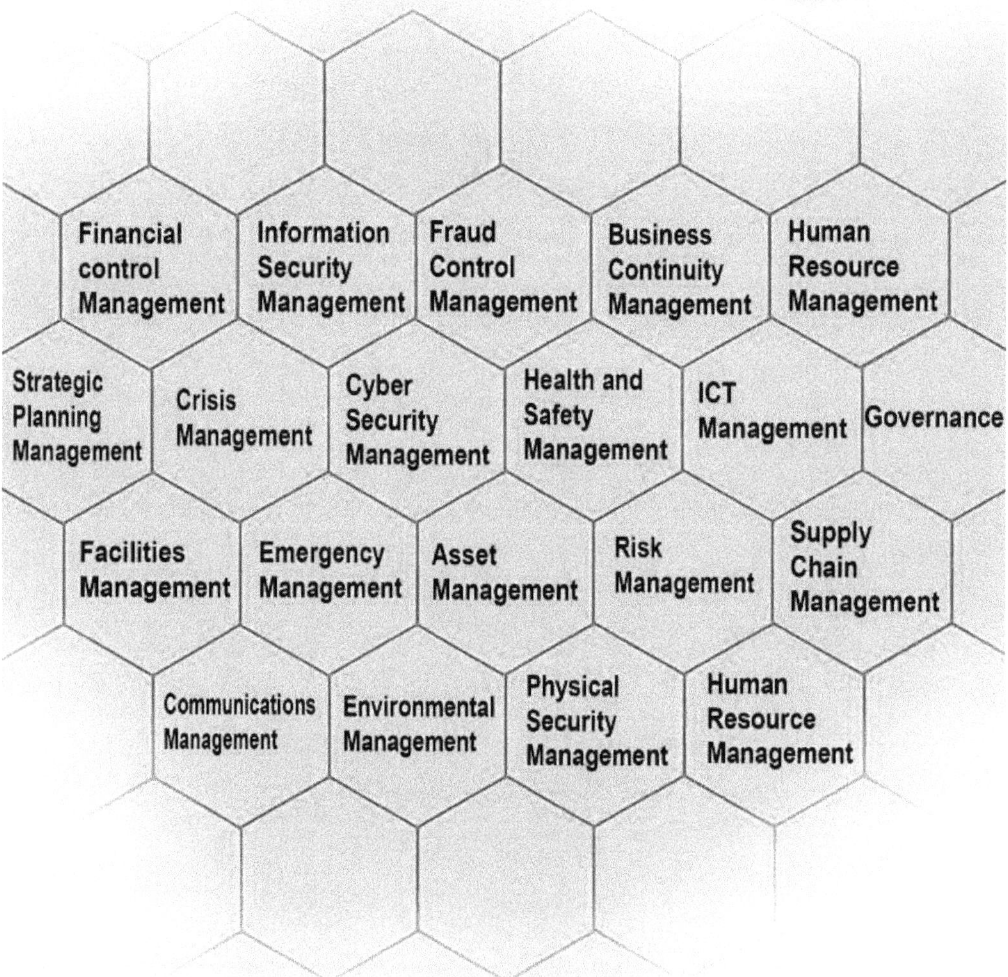

My EXPERIMENTS with
~~TRUTH~~ ORGANISATIONAL RESILIENCE
Part-1

DAMAN DEV SOOD

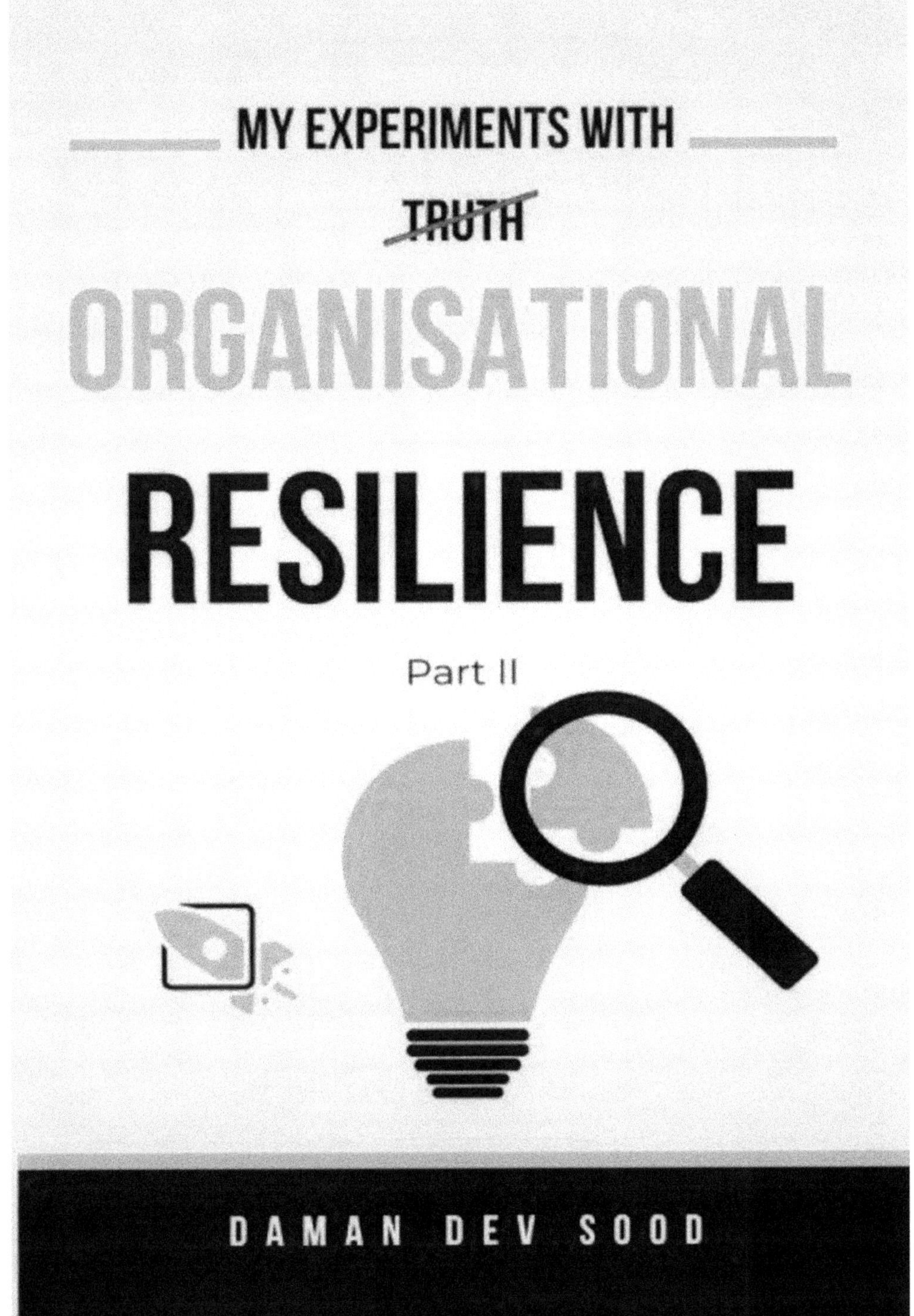
MY EXPERIMENTS WITH
TRUTH
ORGANISATIONAL
RESILIENCE
Part II
DAMAN DEV SOOD

DAMAN DEV SOOD

RESILIENCE
THROUGH THE EYES OF MY READERS

Multiple awards winning Author, Trainer, Consultant,
Speaker, Auditor, Assessor, Researcher

10x
Performance Enhancement
Made Easy
DAMAN DEV SOOD
Delivering Excellence in Project & Program
Management and for Customer Delight

50+ Edible Adventures for Families

Bhavna Sood
Daman Dev Sood

projects your kids can make and eat

My Experiments as a LinkedIn TOP VOICE

Prof. Daman Dev Sood

A mini-Encyclopedia for Consultants, Management Consultants, and Resilience Professionals

Must Read Articles

[i] https://www.linkedin.com/pulse/stakeholder-influence-matrix-business-coaching-tool-chandan-patary/

[ii] https://www.gartner.com/reviews/market/it-vendor-risk-management-solutions/vendor/ibm/product/ibm-openpages-with-watson/alternatives

[iii] https://www.deloitte.com/global/en/services/risk-advisory/blogs/redefining-the-use-of-third-party-management-with-gen-ai.html

[iv] https://www.unilever.com/files/92ui5egz/production/16cb778e4d31b81509dc5937001559f1f5c863ab.pdf

[v] https://stories.starbucks.com/press/2020/cafe-practices-starbucks-approach-to-ethically-sourcing-coffee/

www.ingramcontent.com/pod-product-compliance
Lightning Source LLC
Chambersburg PA
CBHW040206110726
48005CB00019B/2914